"Eric Clayton is among th
lights of a new generation
spirituality. *Finding Peace Here and Now* pulses with Clayton's keen gift for storytelling, bridging experiential and theological insight by way of imagination, gently inviting us to probe our own stories for gestures, big and small, of God's unceasing delight in us. To embrace the 'downward mobility of Christ' is to learn how to savor, in light and shadow, the sacred beauty of our own humanity."

—**Christopher Pramuk**, Regis University Chair
of Ignatian Thought and Imagination

"Braiding together deep research and personal insight, Eric Clayton expertly guides us on a twofold path toward both internal peace and peace in the world around us. Newcomers to Ignatian spirituality as well as those who have practiced it for years will find fresh and engaging inspiration and consolation in these pages. In an age when peace feels especially hard to come by, Clayton assures us that there is wisdom and guidance to be found in our most cherished traditions and, if we listen closely enough, within ourselves."

—**Cameron Bellm**, speaker and author

"In this timely book, Eric Clayton, a gifted and talented writer, mines the five-hundred-year-old Ignatian tradition to meet the demanding needs of peace today. He takes us on a spiritual journey that both inspires and challenges readers to reimagine how we relate to ourselves, to our God, and to one another. Speaking to everything from inner calm to social justice, Clayton's book offers practical tools for any peace seeker in a quest that touches all aspects of our lives."

—**James Martin, SJ**, author of *Learning to Pray:
A Guide for Everyone*

"Eric Clayton's authentic voice emerges in *Finding Peace Here and Now*. If you are overwhelmed by the suffering and complexity in the world, this book offers inspiration and tools to turn our desire for peace into reality by looking at concrete ways we can live as peacemakers in our daily lives. Clayton reminds us that while we cannot change the world, we can allow God to animate our actions, empower us to use our gifts, and begin the work of peace today."

—Becky Eldredge, Ignatian-trained spiritual director, award-winning author, and founder of Ignatian Ministries

"The gifts of Ignatian spirituality—discernment, integration, self-examination, justice—are in short supply in the church today. Now more than ever, we need teachers who can cast a vision for a maturing Christian faith. Eric Clayton is one of those teachers. Here, he turns his attention toward that elusive word we all want but don't know how to get: *peace*. Not only does Clayton show us how to nurture peace within ourselves, he also shows us how to use it to protect others. This book is both salve and sword."

—Shannon K. Evans, author of *The Mystics Would Like a Word: Six Women Who Met God and Found a Spirituality for Today*

"Eric Clayton provides a spiritual road map to finding and fostering peace within our hearts and in the world. A skillful storyteller, Clayton melds personal experiences with the wisdom of the Ignatian tradition, revealing that to be a healing presence we must act justly and seek the *magis* that lies at the heart of our very being—uniting ourselves with God and neighbor so that all may be one. Packed full of prayer prompts and grounds for reflection, *Finding Peace Here and Now* is the book our world (and your spirit) needs now!"

—Sister Colleen Gibson, SSJ, pastoral associate and cohost of the *Beyond the Habit* podcast

Finding Peace
Here and Now

Finding Peace
Here and Now

HOW IGNATIAN SPIRITUALITY
LEADS US TO HEALING
AND WHOLENESS

Eric A. Clayton

Brazos Press

a division of Baker Publishing Group
Grand Rapids, Michigan

Published by Brazos Press
a division of Baker Publishing Group
Grand Rapids, Michigan
BrazosPress.com

Printed in the United States of America

Library of Congress Cataloging-in-Publication Data
Names: Clayton, Eric A., author.
Title: Finding peace here and now : how Ignatian spirituality leads us to healing and wholeness / Eric A. Clayton.
Description: Grand Rapids, Michigan : Brazos Press, a division of Baker Publishing Group, [2025] | Includes bibliographical references.
Identifiers: LCCN 2024045348 | ISBN 9781587436574 (paperback) | ISBN 9781587436734 (casebound) | ISBN 9781493450244 (ebook)
Subjects: LCSH: Ignatius, of Loyola, Saint, 1491–1556. Exercitia spiritualia. | Spiritual life—Catholic Church. | Spiritual exercises.
Classification: LCC BX2179.L8 C53 2025 | DDC 248.088/282—dc23/eng/20241123
LC record available at https://lccn.loc.gov/2024045348

Cover design and art by Kathleen Lynch / Black Kat Design

The author is represented by WordServe Literary Group, www.wordserveliterary.com.

Baker Publishing Group publications use paper produced from sustainable forestry practices and postconsumer waste whenever possible.

25 26 27 28 29 30 31   7 6 5 4 3 2 1

In memory of Father Jim Bowler, SJ,
who believed in this project and believed in me.
Thank you for your guidance, your wisdom,
and your friendship.

Contents

Introduction

A Prayer for Peace

This book is a prayer for peace. We're used to asking God for things. Clear skies on our wedding day. A healthy newborn. Recovery from an earthquake or strength to face a cancer diagnosis. We ask for a successful surgery, a new job, a B+ on our physics test. If you're like me, prayers of petition are your go-to form: *God, please help me . . .* Just add peace to the list, right?

We hear the words often enough: *We pray for peace in our streets. Peace in the face of war. Peace in our hearts and heads. Peace in our relationships.* The words are easy to say. Even now, you might find the names of people and places coming to the forefront of your mind—people and places in need of peace.

My mom used to joke that you never pray for patience. "God won't just *give* you patience," she'd say. "God will give you opportunities to *practice* it. And who has the patience for that!"

Prayer is more than an outcome. And God is not a magician. Rather than waving a hand and making our wishes come true, God desires to draw us into relationship, a relationship that helps us discover who we are and what we're about. Prayer

1

is how we enter into and maintain that relationship. It is a spiritual journey of many steps and seasons. We reach out in faith, extending our hand, unsure of where we will be led—but trusting all the same.

And God takes our hand. God walks with us. God wants to journey together—into the depths of our very selves and out into the vastness of God's awe-inspiring cosmos. God wants us to know that we are beloved.

My mom was right. That which we desire demands our full collaboration. We need to put our prayers of petition into action, trusting that God desires to work with us in the realization of what we seek. I believe that our deepest desires and longings are in fact God's will for us; God has placed these yearnings in the fabric of our beings because God wills that we respond to the moment as only we can. If I desire to work for peace, I believe that's God desiring peace *through me*. God wills that we bring our unique insights, experiences, hopes, and hurts to bear in order to build the world God dreams of.

But this work takes time. It takes focused attention on our daily lived reality because so often it is in the details of our days that we encounter God at work. Through the patterns of our lives, we discover *how* God works in and through us. We discover *why* we desire what we desire; we begin to understand where our passions come from. What might this mean for peace in our world?

Peace isn't something we hope for in a disengaged sort of way. We don't wring our hands together and wish peace into existence. If peace is what we desire—the fruit of our prayer—then we need to practice it.

If we pray for peace, God will give us the opportunities we need to realize it. This book is about recognizing such opportunities—in ourselves, in our communities, in our world—and then seizing them and manifesting God's peace in the present moment.

The great peace activist and Catholic priest John Dear writes in his book *Living Peace: A Spirituality of Contemplation and Action*, "Peace begins within each of us. It is a process of repeatedly showing mercy to ourselves, forgiving ourselves, befriending ourselves, accepting ourselves, and loving ourselves. As we learn to appreciate ourselves and accept God's gift of peace, we begin to radiate peace and love to others."[1]

Peace isn't an abstract thing. Peace is here, now, waiting.

What Is Ignatian Spirituality?

I write in the Ignatian tradition.

Ignatius of Loyola was a Basque soldier. In 1521 he was gravely wounded by a French cannonball strike while defending the castle at Pamplona in northern Spain. The injury forced him to lie in bed, recovering, for eleven months. During that time, Ignatius's own prayer—his own experience of God—demanded that he reevaluate the priorities guiding his life.

Was he fulfilled as a soldier, as a man about court? Or was God calling him to something more? When he daydreamed about chivalric exploits, fighting foes and wooing women, he was left feeling empty. But as he grew in his understanding of God, of God's people, of the role he might play in realizing God's dream for the world, he found something else stirring within him: consolation, inner peace.

As a result, he made a decision: He put down his sword and picked up a pilgrim staff. He set aside a clear symbol of violence and instead devoted his life to discerning the will of God. What was God's great dream for him? Would its pursuit bring peace to his life—and through his life, to the world? That decision set him on a new path. He penned the Spiritual Exercises, the fruit of his own spiritual journey and of his own understanding of God's work in his life.

The Spiritual Exercises eventually evolved into a four-week guided retreat: a series of meditations and exercises that a retreatant would pray through under the guidance of a spiritual director. The director's task is not to instruct; rather, the director's role is that of a companion and spiritual mentor, someone the retreatant can walk with as they progress along their own spiritual journey. The Spiritual Exercises are particularly useful in helping a retreatant discern their vocation and make concrete decisions in their life, grounded always in the understanding that each of us is first and foremost called to praise, reverence, and serve God. To this day, the Spiritual Exercises continue to help spiritual seekers discover something new about themselves and their role in the world. This guided retreat is the foundation of the spirituality that bears Ignatius's name—and the inner journey it lays out has changed the lives of people of all faiths and no faith.

Ignatius wanted more and more people to encounter God through these Exercises. His charisma and devotion attracted many friends and followers, and he eventually helped found the Society of Jesus, more commonly known as the Jesuits, a worldwide order of Catholic priests and brothers.

Ignatius, the soldier-turned-saint, may seem an odd choice for the pursuit of a spirituality of peace. After all, as we will discover, much of the Spiritual Exercises rely on imagery of war and conflict. What else would we expect from a man who had for so long relied on the strength of his sword for his survival and sense of self-worth? As we progress through this book on our own pilgrimage of peace, I will challenge a common assumption that Ignatian spirituality is necessarily too dependent on war imagery to be at all useful for peace work. I will argue instead that Ignatian spirituality is a wellspring of spiritual tools and practices to help us realize peace in our world today. The Exercises, like all things, come from a particular time and place.

Ignatius himself—his own journey, the fruit of his own prayer—offers us an invitation: What are the swords that we clutch so tightly? What are the daydreams that distract us from God's voice whispering in our ear? Once we put those swords down and pick up our own pilgrim staffs, what changes might spread from that singular, seemingly simple decision? How might our decision affect the world?

Why Write About Peace?

Why did I feel the need to write this book—and why now? I've long been intrigued by peace studies. I loved the opportunity I had to collaborate with professional peacebuilders when I worked at Catholic Relief Services, an international humanitarian and development agency. I studied peacebuilding in graduate school and wrote about the role of faith-based actors. I wanted to be a peacebuilder. I wanted that line on my resume.

Why? Quite simply, it's an important, compelling job. And it's just cool: negotiating deals that prevent conflict or end war, that reconcile enemies and bridge opposing perspectives. I wanted to do that. In many ways, I still do.

After years of failing to achieve this goal, I finally realized something: We're *all* called to this work, whether or not it pays our bills. The call to peace is there for each of us; it's just up to us to answer in our unique contexts.

Look at the world: wars hot and cold in countless countries; gang violence in city streets the world over; headlines that report division, dissolution, and discontent in communities near and far. We need peace—and we need it now.

But it wasn't a series of news reports that inspired this book; it was the discovery that *I* lacked peace. Anger, anxiety, frustration, and jealousy—these are emotions that rob me of peace, that turn me against my family and friends. I realized that if these emotions have such power over me, then what's true for me is likely true for others. If we're called to the work of peace but haven't properly examined our own instances of internal *un*peace, then can peace anywhere else truly be achieved? How, then, to approach these wayward emotions?

I've heard sermons that insist the answer lies in waging spiritual warfare against the parts of ourselves that we dislike: anxiety, jealousy, fear, and so on. We should attack these parts and drive them out. But I don't think that can be the answer— certainly not if we're hoping to achieve peace. How can self-inflicted violence nurture in us a spirit of peace?

Anyone who has taken this route likely knows that when we try to destroy a part of ourselves that we dislike, it reappears somewhere down the road. We are who we are; our parts are here to stay. Rather than wage war against them, I believe it's better to befriend them. Understand them. Repair and restore and integrate them. Turn to yourself in peace, not conflict.

Anxiety in my life can cause a lot of harm. It distracts me from the present, clouds my mind and occasionally my judgment. But that same anxious instinct has often reminded me about a forgotten task, ensured the doors were locked at night, and double-checked that my girls have their lunches packed. I don't want to destroy my anxiety; I don't want to chase it away. I want to befriend it, understand it, make it whole.

That's where I begin in the writing of this book, from an inner place that needs peace. Violence is not the answer; it only begets more violence. I don't want to become trapped in an ongoing cycle of "fighting" my anxiety. And I don't want that for you either—whatever your own struggle. I believe that finding peace within is the only way we can ever find peace outside ourselves: among our family, community, nation, and world.

Ignatian spirituality has the tools we need to do exactly that.

Our Path Ahead

This book follows the spiritual path Ignatius mapped out in his Spiritual Exercises, and each chapter ends with a spiritual exercise that will help you practice themes of Ignatian spirituality. If you are familiar with or currently praying through the Exercises, this book will be a helpful companion. If you are unfamiliar with the Exercises or are completely new to Ignatian spirituality, this book is your entry point, an introduction to a new, rich way of encountering God and God's dream for our world.

The first two chapters, much like the preparatory work for anyone doing the Exercises, invite you to meditate on God's unique dream for you, God's will for your life, and your identity before God and God's people. Chapters 3–10 then journey along the traditional path of the Exercises. I highlight key meditations from each of the four so-called weeks—think spiritual movements—and examine them through the lens of peace. Chapters 3 and 4 examine the chaos, suffering, and violence in our world and invite you, the reader, to look clearly and honestly at its effects in your life. Chapters 5–8 dive deeply into the life and ministry of Jesus, following Ignatius's invitation in the Second Week of the Exercises. We learn from Christ how peace and Ignatian principles can both inform our life choices and help us unravel the hidden forces of violence and evil present in our world. Chapters 9 and 10 center on the passion and resurrection of Jesus—the themes of the Third and Fourth Weeks of the Exercises, respectively.

Finally, chapters 11 and 12 sketch out two spiritual practices— creativity and forgiveness—that flow naturally from the Ignatian tradition and can serve us and our world in the work of peace. Often, those who complete the Exercises don't know what to do next to live out what they've learned in prayer; these final two chapters offer two concrete suggestions.

My hope is that if you are currently praying or have prayed the Exercises, this book will add new depth and insight to your experience. My hope, too, is that if you are new to Ignatian spirituality, this book inspires you to go deeper, to learn more and perhaps make the Exercises yourself. Ultimately, my greatest hope is that regardless of your familiarity with the Ignatian tradition, this book becomes a valuable tool in your own vocation as a peacebuilder.

Let me be clear about something up front: This is not an academic inquiry into peacebuilding, though I do pull from both academics and practitioners in that field. This is not a theological treatise either, though you'll hear from theologians. This book is simply an offering I share with you, accompanying my own firm belief that peace is something we need in ways we don't fully realize, and that Ignatian spirituality has something potent and powerful to offer. Though I've written the words you'll find in the following pages, I still struggle to live out their truest meaning. As I revisit and revise these pages, I realize how far I have yet to go in my own quest for peace. And so, as I share the offering of these words with you, my reader, know that we are truly journeying together, companions on the same road. Trust that, while my experiences and reflections may be the ones relayed in the text in your hands, *your* experiences, *your* reflections, *your* unique insights have just as much to teach and contribute to the path of peace. God is at work in your life as God is at work in mine.

Now, as we begin this journey, we return to our prayer of petition. Saint Ignatius encourages us to ask for the grace we desire. It's not a magic trick; we shouldn't expect the fruit of our prayer neatly packaged and delivered to our front porch.

Rather, if we begin this journey—if we ask for the grace of *peace*—we should prepare ourselves for the arduous spiritual work it will demand. Peace isn't simply the absence of conflict; it's a complete reorientation of our relationships. It's not enough to stop harming one another; the peace we're seeking here is one that proactively builds something new, that weaves together the lives of the oppressed and the oppressor into a novel way of living. We put down our weapons, yes, but we also pick up the tools we need to construct a better world. We ask what prevents each of us from achieving our fullest potential—and then we break those obstacles into a million little pieces. This kind of peace is a challenge to the societal structures we take for granted. It demands that we examine closely the words we use, the causes we support, the way we carry ourselves in the world.

Peace isn't reserved for diplomats and humanitarian workers. Peace is for all of us—office staff and elementary-school teachers and soccer coaches and construction workers.

Peace is a challenge. It's a reordering of things, a desire to better mirror God's dream for our lives: a dream built on justice and compassion, one in which every aspect of creation can flourish. And so we pray for peace, yes. We should ask God for the grace of peace.

But I think, as the Ignatian tradition says, we do well to start by asking God for the desire *to desire* peace. God's peace. We can't know where this journey will end. We can't know what it will demand of us—what sacrifices we may need to make, what discoveries about ourselves and our vocations we may stumble upon. It's a leap of faith.

Our desire *to desire* peace is a recognition that we are not God. We don't want to put limits on God's dream of peace. We can't know all that peace will entail. Rather, we want to make ourselves available to being surprised by God, surprised by the Spirit breathing something new into our hearts and minds.

We desire that which we do not know, that which we cannot name, but we know God dreams of peace. So we dare to as well.

CHAPTER 1

God Dreams of More

Discovering Our *Magis*

My younger daughter was born into a tumultuous time in history, so I like to think my distraction was understandable.

A global pandemic had just begun to ravage the world. In the United States, it had been three months since we'd been sent home from work—indefinitely. It was a serendipitous opportunity to spend more time with my family of three before becoming a family of four, but even that joy was laced with uncertainty. Would I be able to be present at my wife's side when our daughter was born? Would we be masked the whole time? Would I be able to *leave* the hospital to check on our older daughter, at home with my parents—and if so, could I then return to the hospital? This was a period riddled with unanswered questions.

But COVID-19 was not the only pandemic unraveling the threads of our society. My daughter was born less than two weeks after the murder of George Floyd at the hands of a Minneapolis police officer. Yet another killing of an unarmed Black man by law enforcement had rattled the nation and stirred people to action. Countless protesters took to the streets demanding meaningful change—and justice.

And all the while, I paced helplessly in a hospital room just outside Baltimore, scrolling through social media. What could I do? What did the moment demand of *me*? I felt inadequate.

My daughter arrived in the middle of the night, healthy, happy, and hungry. By morning my wife was resting, our newborn comfortably nestled in her arms. My task was to call down to the cafeteria to see just when our breakfast would be arriving.

The task was a small one, insignificant against the backdrop of a global pandemic and protests for racial justice. The medical staff of the very hospital in which I stood was on the front lines of securing a healthy and safe future just by doing their regular jobs. Only a few miles away, activists and everyday folks marched through the streets of downtown Baltimore.

All I could do was follow it all in silence, one anxiety-ridden thumb scroll at a time. My wife slept. My baby slept. I paced.

Have you been there? Have you, too, looked out at the world and felt extremely small, unfit to meet the moment, unable to respond in a way that made any real difference? It eats away at you.

There's a scene in *Star Wars: Episode V—The Empire Strikes Back* where Yoda, the shriveled old Jedi master, scolds a young Luke Skywalker. Luke is unable to focus, refuses to be mindful and present. He's anxious to begin his Jedi training, to find the renowned Jedi master he's come to learn from. The time spent with this mysterious green figure in a swamp hovel is time wasted, to Luke's mind. He grows impatient, angry.

That's when Yoda reveals himself to be the one Luke seeks— but not before getting a dig in: "All his life has he looked away . . . to the future. . . . Never his mind on where he was. . . . What he was doing."[1] Yoda fears that such inner turmoil would lead Luke down the path of the dark side, as it had his father.

That was me in that hospital room: looking away to a different moment, unable to sink into the present beauty in which I found myself. I was too busy imagining the roles I *wasn't* playing, some of which I wasn't even qualified for: activist, marcher, health-care worker, advocate, lawyer. I was afraid that the "big" needs of the moment would pass me by, that I wouldn't be enough to meet them. I was afraid I wouldn't be seen by others and myself as trying, as playing my part.

I had no inner peace. I had nothing but turmoil and inadequacy and a sense of missing out.

But what I was really missing was the *actual* need of the moment, the actual roles I was being asked to fill: father, husband, companion, partner, procurer of breakfast.

Take a moment and think about similar places you've stood, places where your feet have been while your mind has been pulled in a million other directions. What kept you from the inner peace you no doubt desired? What were you afraid of missing?

Too often, this misalignment between who we think we need to become and who the moment is asking us to be brings nothing but inner turmoil. In this chapter, we'll begin to uncover some Ignatian spiritual tools to close the gap between who we are right now and who we might yet grow into.

We Want More

Ignatius of Loyola begins the Spiritual Exercises with a meditation called the First Principle and Foundation. It serves as an invitation to the one going through the Exercises—the exercitant or retreatant—to seek out and embody the will of God. In so doing, the exercitant becomes indifferent to all other things, holding them loosely, always ready to let go of or embrace whatever will more readily bring about God's dream for that person and the world.

"We must make ourselves indifferent to all created things," Ignatius writes. "As far as we are concerned, we should not prefer health to sickness, riches to poverty, honor to dishonor, a long life to a short life."[2] No matter the situation in which we find ourselves, no matter the context of our life, we desire to manifest God's will.

Easy, right?

In the abstract, this reads like marriage vows. How blissfully we enter into them amid the fanfare of our wedding day! Surrounded by family and friends and a night of feasting and celebrating ahead, how can we think of anything *but* health and good times? Sickness? Bad times? They're for after we've digested the cake. We say we're committed to our beloved "for better, for worse," but as far as we can see, it's all better, no worse.

As anyone who has entered into any sort of committed relationship knows, the good times do not last; the glimmer of young love fades. What remains is that commitment, the foundation built by two people determined to muddle through life—in all its mystery and unknowns and wonder and awe and challenge—together.

So, too, in these first lines of the Exercises. This is why the final line of the First Principle and Foundation is essential: "Our one desire and choice should be what is more conducive to the end for which we are created."[3]

That word *more* is where we get the Ignatian spiritual principle *magis*. *Magis* is the Latin word for *more*. I've seen it in several advertisements at Jesuit-run schools and institutions. *Magis* is interpreted as a challenge to be more, do more, accomplish more. More push-ups, more internships, more track records of academic and professional success.

It's not wrong to work to become more. It is, however, incomplete.

What *magis* means here goes beyond a great job offer or another basketball championship. It's not doing more for the sake of doing more. You're not becoming the best simply to say you did. Ignatius wants us to pursue the ends for which we are uniquely made. When Ignatius says *more*, he means more of the unique God-stuff that makes up you and me. God desires we love and serve God and God's people as *only we can.*

Want to seek the *magis*? Become more authentically *you.*

Focusing on becoming a more authentic you is what makes relationships work. It's what brings out professional success. We become more and more aware of who we really are, what makes us tick, why we do the things we do. Understanding ourselves helps us better understand others because we know who we are and who we're not. We begin to put aside judgment, envy, pride. We don't fear the opinions or success of others because we know that we are not meant to be *them*—we're meant to be *us.*

Our one desire is to be ever more the person we already are. We go deeper into ourselves and there encounter the whole universe—and our place within it. In the words of the great Canadian Jesuit John English, we enter our "life story as an expression of God's unique personal love for" us; we seek "to attain a reflective knowledge of God's unique love for us."[4] Go ahead and underline that word *unique*. God deals with us in all our distinctiveness; it is in the *stuff* of our utterly exceptional selves that our own *magis* shines forth. Prayer can be simply God's opportunity to remind us of our uniqueness. Then, with God, we bask in this simple fact: We are wonderfully made (Ps. 139:14).

God delights in us simply for who we are, and we in turn savor God's loving gaze. Is this not the peace we seek?

I think back to that hospital room. I had no inner peace because I had reduced *magis* to simply *more*. I wanted to be *more than I was made for in that moment*: an activist on the street, a doctor despite my squeamishness around blood, a legislator writing new laws.

I was looking beyond the moment, beyond my own experiences and abilities and context. I wasn't sinking into myself. Instead, I was afraid of who I wasn't—and I was letting fear rob me of any peace.

The French Jesuit priest and scientist Pierre Teilhard de Chardin writes, "The deeper I descend into myself, the more I find God at the heart of my being . . . the God who pursues in me the task, as endless as the whole sum of centuries, of the incarnation of his Son."[5] Just as God entered human history in a particular way in the Incarnation, the birth of Jesus, so too does God continue to enter into the human story through our lives. We are unique expressions of the body of Christ. Becoming ever more who God knows we can be manifests ever more clearly our singular part in Christ's body. This is the *magis*: a recognition that our very selves contain something essential to God and God's world—and understanding that "something" as a constant, unfurling mystery. There is always more of us to know and understand, and the more we do so, the more we can fully and authentically live out our part in God's creation.

But first, we have to see the world around us—and our unique place in it—as it really is. In that moment in that hospital room, my *magis* lay in simply being present to my newborn child and to my wife. Nothing more, nothing less. When I realized that, when I sank into that moment, into who I was called to be, I glimpsed the peace I sought. I held my daughter; I brought breakfast to my wife. Simple, meaningful, personal tasks.

Peace can only be found where we already are. Anything else is a distraction from the moment, from the people who need you here and now.

Necessary Limitations

You might be thinking, "Eric, it sounds like you're saying to accept the status quo. Never change. You are what you are, and that's it. There's no reason to dream or grow or work for a world that benefits people you may never meet."

I hear you, but nothing is further from the truth. A disposition toward growth, change, and transformation is foundational to any spiritual journey.

But we don't find or manifest peace by obsessing over what we are not *yet*, what we have not *yet* become. The enemy of our human nature—to borrow an Ignatian expression—wants nothing more than to distract us from the needs of the moment, the people right there in front of us. Our attention becomes splintered; we become that much less present to the people before us and that much less useful to the world at large. We are emotionally, mentally, and spiritually torn apart.

At the same time, these whispers that beckon us deeper into our most authentic self and then beyond ourselves into the needs of the world are worth paying attention to. These whispers speak to us of our values, of what drives us and gets us out of bed in the morning, of what we profess to be important. Within these nudges our desires are reflected, the inklings of who we might yet become. Desires are foundational to Ignatian spirituality. Ignatius believed that through our desires, God speaks. God invites. God shows us our vocations.

Here's the important part: We *pay attention* to these whispers; we don't *give* them our attention. We notice, but we don't allow ourselves to be consumed. We stand in the present moment, in all of its unique context, and ask *who we are called to be here, now.* As we respond to that call, next steps emerge. God speaks to us through our desires, our values, our hopes and dreams, and the people around us. But these desires are grounded in a particular time, place, community, and set of experiences.

As such, we must accept our necessary limitations based on the moment. All things are possible for God, but we are bound by the limitations of our reality. We evolve slowly, steadily from our particular place; we cannot rush who we are becoming. We make choices that necessarily take other choices off the table.

I'm a writer, not a surgeon, because I spend and have spent time improving my writing craft; I've not spent any time learning how to do surgery—which is probably for the best. Nothing in my past hints at a future in surgery. I was terrible at high school biology, blood makes me queasy, and I never once thought to fill college electives with science courses. I can spend my time admiring surgeons, being grateful for the work they do—and I can do so confidently, knowing that pursuing my *magis* means expressing that gratitude and then turning back to *deepening my own vocation*. Wondering about what I might have accomplished as a surgeon, wishing for that life, trying to force myself to study anatomy now without any real desire, interest, or past experience in the field makes little sense.

This is perhaps an extreme example. You might even be shaking your head, saying, "Eric, *I'm* a surgeon *and* a great writer!" But here's the point: That's *you*, in all your unique glory: context, passion, experience. Still, there are probably areas in your life, as there are in mine, where you are tempted to give your attention to things that are wholly unrealistic or unnecessary, but you do so because, rather than wanting the *magis*, you simply want *more*. You want to fill the résumé, fill the day, feel ful*filled* based on a variety of roles and activities—rather than being filled by being who and what you are now.

Ultimately, *magis* means simply becoming more you, and you can only do so much. But you can be everything you need to be here, now.

"Be who you are and be that well," is a saying commonly attributed to Saint Francis de Sales. Don't worry about being someone else; don't surrender your peace of mind, heart, and spirit to fulfill someone else's unique purpose. Saint Irenaeus says something to the effect of, "The glory of God is a human being fully alive."[6] You are only as fully alive as you are uniquely *you*.

You Are the One You've Been Waiting For

If you've watched Disney's *Frozen II*, as I have countless times, then you know that the plot loosely centers on Queen Elsa's search for the source of a mysterious voice. She hypothesizes that finding the voice will also help her solve a host of other elemental problems plaguing Arendelle and the surrounding region.

Elsa is so obsessed with finding this other thing that she pushes her friends aside, puts herself in danger, and very nearly ruins everything she's worked for. The search consumes her. What she ultimately discovers—in the form of my youngest daughter's favorite song, "Show Yourself"—is a simple truth: "You are the one you've been waiting for."

In true Disney-princess fashion, this transformation from not knowing to knowing is represented by a change in wardrobe: Elsa's dress turns icy white with an accent of blue. She puts on something new that fits her perfectly; it looks totally different and yet like something she'd wear. It brings out something new about her, something *more*, while still staying true to who this character already is.

Elsa's discovery, naturally, saves the day and without a moment to spare. She grows more and more into who she is meant to be, stepping down as queen but stepping up and into a new role, one that is reflective of the elemental powers she discovered *she had all along.*

Much to my daughters' chagrin, we don't live in a Disney movie. We can't get Elsa powers that let us blast icy cold magic. But similar to Elsa, each of us can gaze deeply at ourselves— past, present, and future—and know with confidence that God's Spirit dwells within us. There's no moment when the Spirit begins dwelling within us; there's no threat that we'll lose the Spirit. We are God's dwelling place, full stop.

Yet how many of us really feel that truth? We may know it intellectually from years of Sunday school, but do we let it affect who we are, how we live, how we see ourselves in the world? Do we hear the Spirit whispering urgently, "You are enough. You are what I had in mind all along. You are becoming exactly who I hoped you'd be"? We may not don a princess gown to reflect our spiritual discoveries; we likely look exactly as we did before, but something might feel different, if even for a moment. We rest in the knowledge of God's Spirit uniquely at work in us.

Inner peace is found when we become more authentically who we already are. Inner peace is found when we hear that voice—and listen.

In Suspense and Incomplete

I spent a year of postgraduate service in Bolivia. While there, I was surrounded by downright impressive volunteers. One friend was beloved by all the kids—he was tall and strong and able to play all sorts of fun games. Another spoke perfect Spanish and so was able to go deep quickly with members of the community, offering insight, consolation, and laughter. Still another was particularly extroverted and able to insert herself into any situation with confidence, a leader able to bring comfort and joy just by being herself.

Then there was me. I was introverted, spoke poor Spanish, and was no good at the games any of the kids wanted to play. I saw in my fellow volunteers everything that I was not. *Why am I even here? What am I even adding? I wish I were more like . . .*

It took me a long time to realize that two things could be true: I was enough in that moment, and I didn't need to be what my fellow volunteers were *yet*. I could learn from them, appreciate their virtues and skills, and grow into such traits in my own way, in my own time.

As it turned out, the extroverted volunteer often turned to me for my opinion. Some of the quieter kids enjoyed playing games with me—probably *because* I didn't attract such a gaggle of children. And while my Spanish never was good enough for deep conversations, I had many profound conversations with the Bolivian English teachers at the local school. My fellow volunteers met the needs of the community by being themselves—and so did I.

In the Spiritual Exercises, Ignatius gives us what he calls the Presupposition. It's meant as a rule of thumb to guide the relationship between the retreat director and the exercitant. Ignatius writes, "It is necessary to suppose that every good Christian is more ready to put a good interpretation on another's statement than to condemn it as false."[7] In short, Ignatius asks us to give one another—not just Christians—the benefit of the doubt, trusting that we are all doing our best and that God is still at work.

Sometimes it's easier for us to give others the benefit of the doubt than it is to give it to ourselves. But I believe Ignatius is asking that of us too. As we learn and grow and become both more who we already are and who we are yet meant to be, we need to be gentle with ourselves. We need to give ourselves grace, allowing God to work in God's time.

Peace is about living in that creative tension between pursuing your *magis* and resting in the present and Presence. Becoming who you are *here*, *now*, and allowing your desires to carry you one step at a time to manifest who you are becoming. Always learning from those who inspire in you compassion and love, while withholding judgment of self or neighbor.

Being kind to yourself dispels the fear of not being enough. We then look to others with love and curiosity, not shame, insecurity, or envy.

That same French Jesuit scientist, Pierre Teilhard de Chardin, wrote a prayer called "Patient Trust" that sums this up well. I encourage you to pray it—and see if you can more deeply enter into that creative tension, that paradox of self that both *is* and is *still becoming*. The more you come to know that self, the more peace you will have for yourself and to share with others.

Patient Trust

Above all, trust in the slow work of God.
We are quite naturally impatient in everything to reach
the end without delay.
We should like to skip the intermediate stages.
We are impatient of being on the way to something un-
known, something new.

And yet it is the law of all progress
that it is made by passing through some stages of
instability—
and that it may take a very long time.

And so I think it is with you;
your ideas mature gradually—let them grow,
let them shape themselves, without undue haste.
Don't try to force them on,
as though you could be today what time
(that is to say, grace and circumstances acting on your
own good will)
will make of you tomorrow.

Only God could say what this new spirit
gradually forming within you will be.
Give Our Lord the benefit of believing
that his hand is leading you,
and accept the anxiety of feeling yourself
in suspense and incomplete.[8]

A Spiritual Exercise for Peace Work

Opening Prayer

Pray for the grace to recognize God's delight in who you are now, in this moment, while also recognizing God's dream for who you will become.

Prayer Text

Now the one who has prepared us for this very thing is God, who has given us the Spirit as a first installment.

So we are always courageous, although we know that while we are at home in the body we are away from the Lord, for we walk by faith, not by sight. Yet we are courageous, and we would rather leave the body and go home to the Lord. . . .

So whoever is in Christ is a new creation: the old things have passed away; behold, new things have come. And all this is from God, who has reconciled us to himself through Christ and given us the ministry of reconciliation, namely, God was reconciling the world to himself in Christ, not counting their trespasses against them and entrusting to us the message of reconciliation. So we are ambassadors for Christ, as if God were appealing through us.

2 Corinthians 5:5–8, 17–20

Reflection Exercises

- Do you feel the tension in the Scripture passage? The desire to be present to God in the now while also drawing nearer to who God desires us to be in the future? Do you see such tension reflected in your own life? Does this tension get in the way of your inner peace?

- We feel endlessly burdened with the need to act on God's will in our lives, to surmount those obstacles that prevent us from living God's dream. Yet God has placed us in *this* moment. What might the Spirit be trying to show us about ourselves and our context? What is distracting us from the Spirit's whisper?

Conversation

- In conversation with God or with neighbor, discuss what *magis* means in your life. Ask God to reveal to you how a pursuit of *magis* can help you manifest Christ and live as a "new creation." In your life and context, how does a reorientation toward *magis* breathe something new into your sense of self and relationships?
- What "message of reconciliation" are you being tasked with spreading?

Journal

- Spend time meditating on the "message of reconciliation" that has been uniquely given to you. How have you shared it in the past? How will you share it in the future? How does your own *magis* factor in?

CHAPTER 2

Experience Delight

Embracing Our Identity as Beloved

This chapter begins with a warning: The next few lines contain spoilers for the great 1999 film by M. Night Shyamalan, *The Sixth Sense*. Do you remember that movie? Bruce Willis as child psychologist Dr. Malcolm Crowe. Haley Joel Osment as young Cole Sear.

Even if you didn't see the film, it's likely you know two things about it. First, Osment's Cole sees dead people. That line—"I see dead people"—was riffed on and reinterpreted a million times across pop culture.[1] Second, Willis's character, Dr. Crowe, is dead for the majority of the movie.

I was still in elementary school when the film came out. I remember watching it and having my mind blown by the ending. *The Sixth Sense* holds a special place in the echelons of twist-ending movies. It was a story that permeated the zeitgeist—and plenty of follow-up films tried to recapture the same *You mean to tell me . . . This whole time?!* moment.

The revelation that Willis's character is actually one of the dead people that young Cole sees recasts their relationship. In fact, it recasts every one of Crowe's relationships throughout the film. There's a nice reversal of roles: The patient winds up helping the doctor, and we see how the doctor's self-realization allows for healing, for letting go, for next steps.

But most significantly for viewers, this twist invites us—demands us, even—to watch the movie again. Each line lands differently. *Oh, right—the dead rarely realize they're dead.* Each scene holds new secrets. *I guess Dr. Crowe never actually had that conversation.* Our eyes are open to a paradigm-shifting truth. As a result, the story unfolds in new ways, revealing new and essential insights. We see what's come before in a new light.

That will be the work of this chapter. We're not trying to impose twists and turns in our own stories—I'm sure we each have plenty of those already. No matter where we are in our own life story, God is constantly inviting us to a deeper understanding of who we truly are, in and through our own *magis*, our more. But first, we have to embrace how God sees us.

Quite simply, we are God's beloved. This simple, profound truth can and does radically reorient how we make sense of our own personal history.

We often allow past wounds to fester and drive actions in the present, but we have to find peace, even in the challenging, traumatic moments in our stories. If we don't reexamine and repair and renew those past hardships, we inadvertently carry that same violence and struggle and pain into our present.

God's Beloved

I remember the first time my spiritual director, the late Jesuit priest Jim Bowler, asked if I realized I was God's beloved.

"You know God delights in you, right?"

I paused. Opened my mouth. Closed it again. "What? No." I was only in my second year of undergraduate studies at Fairfield University. I could tell you a lot about the rules of the Catholic Church, but this idea of a God who *delights*? Absolutely not.

"God *delights* in *you*," my Jesuit friend insisted. "Always." I'd never realized it. It never crossed my mind. I could easily name my past sins and errors and missteps and regrets and failures. I was pretty sure God could too.

The notion that God was too busy delighting in me to be caught up in reciting a litany of my mistakes was revelatory.

Father Bowler invited me to pray with Matthew 3, the baptism of the Lord, more than once. "Can you hear God saying those words to *you*?" he asked. "*This is my beloved. You are God's beloved.*"

One of the hallmarks of Ignatian spirituality—and Ignatian contemplation in particular—is the use of the imagination in reading Scripture. Ignatius invites us to place ourselves in the scene. To become one of the characters, or to simply walk alongside Christ or Mary or one of the disciples as we are. Ignatius encourages us to use all our senses as we mentally re-create this moment from Scripture. Can we feel the heat of the sun on our skin? Can we hear the whispers of the crowd? Can we see the vastness of the desert?

We trust that God is at work in our imagination, that the Spirit is filling in the details in a way that is unique to us and our prayer. We enter Scripture as we are, knowing that the experiences, insights, hopes, and challenges of our story will distinctively illuminate and be illuminated by Christ's story.

I invite you to consider the baptism scene from Scripture. To walk with Jesus down to the River Jordan. To feel the rough ground beneath your feet and the curious stares of the gathered crowd at your back. To meet the Baptist himself and to insist on being plunged into the cold, dark water. To feel the wetness against your skin, soaking your clothes. That moment of panic, doubt, shadow as you are completely and totally submerged. And then—the sun once more, the warmth, the relief, the wonder.

And then to hear a voice saying to you, "This is my beloved, with whom I am well pleased."

Is this a twist in your story? It certainly was in mine. Better said, it was a new and essential discovery. It continues to reshape how I understand events in my life. *God delights in me.* Perhaps it's not as exciting as a he-was-dead-the-whole-time twist, but it's powerful and poignant. Seeing ourselves as God's beloved can alter how we understand every aspect of our own lives—if we allow it to.

If God delights in us now, God has delighted in us in the past. God has always delighted in us because we have always been God's beloved. Nothing gets in God's way.

Story over Ending

Nearly every creative writing teacher I've ever had has hated twist endings.

Their thinking goes like this: You've spent all this time building a world, crafting a story, creating characters, only to pull the rug out from under your reader at the end. Too much relies on that moment of discovery at or near the story's conclusion and not enough on the character development that should be taking place throughout the tale. Plus, readers don't like to be lied to.

Even still, we do sometimes like twist endings. Every one of those creative writing teachers also said something to the effect of, "But if you can do it *well*, then . . ."

People return to *The Sixth Sense* even knowing the twist. In fact, we all return to stories again and again. Not because we're expecting to be surprised anew, but because we want to savor the details, to relive the moments, to let them sink into our imaginations and lift our gazes in wonder.

A good twist simply accelerates that process. Again, how many of us needed to rewatch *The Sixth Sense* immediately because we wanted to appreciate the story through the lens of our new knowledge? To see and marvel at the little Easter eggs hidden throughout the film that our he-was-dead-the-whole-time insight reveals with clarity?

I wonder what happens when we apply the same approach to our own life stories. We rest in God's delight. We revel in the knowledge that we are God's beloved. Then we go through the story again. As you go back through the hills and valleys of your own life, what does this new insight reveal? Do you see God at work in surprising ways? Do you begin to recognize the patterns through which the Spirit has been moving in your life, beholding and delighting in you?

The Ignatian tradition invites us to consider our graced history. "A series of events becomes graced history when it is approached and understood in terms of God's constant loving presence with each individual and the whole human race," writes Father John English again from his classic text, *Spiritual Freedom: From an Experience of the Ignatian Exercises to the Art of Spiritual Guidance.*[2] The threads of our own lives, the lives of members of our community and of every community—these stories form a graced history. When we look at these stories through the lens of our relationship to God, how God invites us to follow the path of Christ, we begin to see new details, and we begin to see old details in new ways.

"The main purpose of prayer is to grow in the knowledge of God's love for us so that we may be instruments of that love in our world," Father English writes.[3] We sift through the raw material of our lives *with God* and *with the knowledge of our own belovedness* so as to emerge into the present moment ready and able to live out our unique *magis.*

Praying with our graced history through the lens of God's delight in us can change everything. "We must view God as approving and affirming when we take a spiritual approach to all the events of our life story," English writes. "Knowing that God regards us with unconditional love enables us to recall all the events of our lives, whether they are positive or negative. With reflection we recognize the unique way God relates to us."[4] Remember: It's not about pretending we haven't made mistakes or experienced loss and difficulty; it's about not letting those mistakes consume our focus. Rather, even in those moments of woundedness and worry, we know God still delights in us, still calls us forth, still desires good things for us. And most important of all, God approves and affirms in unconditional love our desire to go back and look at the past moments in our life anew: Even when it's hard. Even when it's uncomfortable. Even when we discover that we weren't always the hero we pretended to be.

Meanwhile, in Bolivia

You might be thinking, "That's all well and good when things go well. But what about when things are tough, when we are in moments of pain and suffering, and the idea of a loving God delighting in us seems farfetched at best?"

We still turn to prayer, to God. "We compose ourselves in faith before God, Scripture, and our life story," Father English tells us. "We pray for the felt knowledge of identity, vocation, or mission. Memory is the instrument of recall, yet this type of prayer is not just for reminiscing, but for being present and finding meaning in the events of our lives."[5] As English implies, sometimes we have to do so well after the events in question have taken place. Finding grace in hardship takes time and distance.

During the many months I lived and served in Bolivia, I struggled. It was not an easy period in my life. Things never quite clicked for me as they did for so many of my friends volunteering both in Bolivia and elsewhere.[6] I never felt that I was enough for the moment. And in part, that's because I assumed I had arrived in the country with all the answers. After all, I was a twenty-something white kid with a bachelor's degree in international studies from a school in New England! Wasn't I destined for postgraduate service? And weren't they lucky to have me? In many ways, I'm embarrassed by the version of myself that showed up in Bolivia. I complained about my living conditions (*I thought I was going to have my own room!*) and about the tasks I was given (*I don't want to teach English; I want to teach religion!*) and about the community in which I found myself (*Why don't these people pray more!*). When things got tough, I didn't know what to do; I wasn't up to the task.

There's one moment in particular that stands out to me. We were on a weeklong field trip visiting an orphanage in a different part of the country. I was assigned to stay with the elementary school boys in a series of adjoining rooms that were little more than concrete cells. One of the boys—I can barely picture him now, but I remember he was cheerful, if subdued, with a mop of brown hair and big brown eyes—had no mattress on his bed. He slept directly on the metal springs. I asked the religious sister who ran the place about this oversight. She told me he'd wet the bed too many times. He'd get his mattress back when he learned better.

What's a twenty-something kid with a fancy degree and an inflated sense of self supposed to do with that? It haunts me still, especially now that I have two daughters of my own, that this five-year-old was sleeping on mattress springs as a form of punishment. The poor kid was probably carrying such trauma that he was utterly overwhelmed. And what did I do? I failed him. I nodded along with that sister, frowning at that kid. I didn't have within me what was needed to meet that moment. All I had was an expectation that I'd be greeted like some savior,

31

fed good local food, and treated to a delightful cultural experience. I wonder still what was truly needed of me in that moment. All I know is it took me much longer than it should have to realize that what I gave then was woefully insufficient.

I've been asked many times if going to Bolivia was the right decision, or if I had somehow discerned incorrectly. Would I do it differently, given the chance? And I wonder: Was there a different volunteer program out there that would have been a better fit, formed me better for what I would face? Should I have spent that year after my undergraduate studies elsewhere or simply known to bring a more enlightened disposition to the experience?

The answer to all these questions is a begrudging, frustrating, and contradictory *yes*. Yes, I could have certainly brought a better disposition, and if I had, who's to say how my year—and my sense of self—would have unfolded? Yes, I could have spent that time elsewhere, and who's to say what opportunities would have arisen if I had? And yes, ultimately, God would have been there, regardless of the choice I made. Just as God was there with me then, even in that cement room, in all it and I lacked, delighting. Remember: Father English insists that our God is always affirming of our serious effort to review our lives—the good, the bad, and the ugly.

And so I wade through those memories and smile, because the people I met, the experiences I had, the insights I gained, and the opportunities that have come as a result of that year are not things I regret. They are all *intrinsic* to my unfolding story. They are part of how I understand myself and my vocation here and now. I can see with increasing clarity the mistakes I made, the arrogance and sense of self-importance with which I arrived in Bolivia. Still, I see more clearly the good desires that brought me to that place, the hope and the determination that landed me in a country not my own. These desires to go out to and be moved by the stories of others, of folks like those who welcomed me in Bolivia. These are desires that reflect a pattern in my life, a pattern in which I trust God to be at work.

These seeds were planted during my undergraduate studies and the many immersion trips I participated in. These seeds have borne good fruit in the story-gathering trips I embark on each year in my professional life and the time I have spent visiting communities around the world, where I uplift voices and ways of life that might otherwise go unheard. Even now, after so many years, I struggle to bring the right disposition. My story, like all of ours, has both light and darkness.

The act of integrating these darker moments into my graced history is a necessary one. The work is still incomplete, as I continue to think back and shake my head at the air of privilege with which I trekked about South America. And yet, I can still see God at work, even in those moments of confusion and hardship. The simple fact that I can look back now and see that little boy at the orphanage for who he was—struggling with trauma, desperate for attention and love, lost but still capable of hope, and most importantly, *the beloved of God*—is, I believe, God at work. God isn't condoning my abhorrent behavior, nor is God giving me a free pass. But the Spirit is inviting me to look more clearly at where I've been, who I've met, and the opportunities I have in the present to make right the mistakes I made in the past as best I can. That moment is part of my story whether I like it or not.

Many people—perhaps you, reading now—have far more traumatic events from their lives that still need to be incorporated into their graced histories. If this describes you, I encourage you to reflect on your story and then begin that work, perhaps one tiny step at a time. At the end of the day, we can confront our painful past or we can ignore it, but what happens when we ignore it? What happens when the wounds continue to fester and old stories are left unchallenged and unexamined?

Are we better off? Or do we allow the seeds of violence and hate to grow in the darkness?

Do Something New

The stories we tell ourselves about ourselves don't just impact us. These stories necessarily pour out, overflow, and flood the lives of those around us, friend and stranger alike. If we embrace our calling as beloved members of God's human family, if we *really* see ourselves as deserving of God's eternal delight, we are inevitably changed. We carry ourselves differently. We know that our *magis* is enough for us and our world, and we are eager and ready to live it. We all know the easy confidence of a person who believes that they are doing exactly what they have been made to do. There is no need to compete or put on airs when you already know you're doing what needs to be done. You have met your moment and continue to do so, simply by being all that you are. Envy, pride, arrogance—these things can fade away.

If we do not see ourselves as beloved—but as lacking, riddled by shame and failure, and living in constant fear of not being enough, doing enough, having enough—then our story takes a different turn. We live looking over our shoulder, comparing ourselves to others. If we don't believe that we are already enough, then we look to tear others down and use the wreckage to build ourselves up.

This plays out in daily life. We compete with colleagues to get the boss's approval. We compete with our neighbors to throw the best parties. We compete with our partners to be seen as the more fun parent. We compete with our peers to be considered the smartest, most competent, or wittiest of our group.

This is human nature. Yet, deep down we are quietly confessing to not feeling wholly sufficient as we already are. We think, *Sure, I'm beloved—but God would love me more if I got this job or that honor or another degree.*

34

It's not bad to want to grow and to challenge ourselves, to learn new things and have new experiences and, through community, become the best versions of ourselves. But we must constantly return to the person we already are, not the person we project ourselves to be. As we do so, as we pray with our own graced history, discovering God delighting in us all along—regardless of our titles, accolades, wealth, or the opinions of others—we become grounded in who we are actually becoming. The patterns in our lives reveal themselves. We become more at ease in our own skin.

In Isaiah 43:19 we read, "See, I am doing something new! Now it springs forth, do you not perceive it?" That new thing is you and me, the complete originality that is our story. That has been our story all along, but too often we don't perceive it. "In the wilderness I make a way, in the wasteland, rivers." I wonder if that wilderness and wasteland is not our own lives at times—or how *we* perceive our lives. God reminds us that we are more than the wilderness or wasteland in which we may feel trapped. God invites us beyond and into our graced history.

When I was a graduate student at American University, I spent time studying religion and peace. I wanted to know how religious traditions play a role in promoting and sustaining true peace in our world. It won't surprise you that to promote peace in the world, religious traditions first need to discover peace within their own texts, institutions, and rituals. We know only too well how easy it is—and how prevalent throughout history—for religious texts to be co-opted by those who wish to do violence, manifest hate, or discriminate against entire communities.

The book that unlocked my own thinking on this topic is called *Globalizing God: Religion, Spirituality and Peace*. The authors, Johan Galtung and Graeme MacQueen, propose four ways for religious communities to grapple with problematic texts, or texts that are easily interpreted for violent ends. We can reject a text as not part of revelation; we can keep the text in the proverbial attic, meaning the text goes unused; we can emphasize the function of a text—for example, recitation in ritual—rather than the literal meaning; and, finally, we can reframe the text.[7]

It's the last response that I find most compelling: the reframing. "To become useful to a religious community, Scripture needs to be interpreted," Galtung and MacQueen write. "The kind of reframing that is needed is the re-contextualizing of the entire body of Scripture so that it is available to the community in a new way."[8]

This approach is important for religious communities, but I mention it here because I believe it to be important for our own work in this chapter. God is doing something new in the world through us, God's beloved. And God desires that we *perceive* it, that we discover those paths in the wilderness and those rivers in the wastelands. We need to see so that we can respond.

Father English writes, "In order to pray with our history we must approach it in the same way that we approach Scripture, that is, as revelation of God's message to us."[9] If we are called to approach our own graced history in the same way we approach our holy texts, then we must embrace the challenge of reframing the scripture of our lives in the context of our belovedness. Of God's constant delight. Of our unique *magis* in this moment in this place.

"The body of texts evolves according to changing needs and circumstances as discerned through the community's changing faithfulness," Galtung and MacQueen note. "The emphasis is on the commitment to *struggle* for such improvement."[10] Are we faithful to a God who delights in us, who sees us as enough? Or are we enthralled by a false god who demands we measure up, compete, acquire, and prove our worth?

Finding our way to this God of constant delight *is* a struggle in a world that insists we divide ourselves into winners and losers.

Give Thanks

So how do we do it? How do we rest and revel in this God of delight, both in the eternal now and in the graced history that is our life story? How do we reframe the holy text of our lives so as to manifest peace to ourselves and our communities in the present? Ignatius of Loyola gives us a prayer called the Examen. Quite simply, it is an invitation to review the day—or any set period of time—in the Spirit. Ignatius suggests we pray this prayer at least once a day. There are five steps. I like to think of them this way:

1. Thanksgiving
2. Light
3. Detail
4. Shadow
5. Onward

We begin in thanksgiving, cultivating a disposition of gratitude toward God and ourselves for the wonders of the day. Next, it may be helpful to address the Holy Spirit as the Spirit of Light, since we are praying to see clearly all that has transpired—and in particular, those places covered in shadow, those times in our lives that are hard to face or that we have pushed out of mind. We ask the Spirit of Light to help us see and recall the moments of our day clearly, to hold each up as a gem glittering in the sun. We review those details carefully, again using our senses to slowly walk through the day's many faces, places, and events. We can progress through our day chronologically or as the Spirit directs. We ask to be made aware of the shadows in our day, those opportunities for growth and development where we might respond differently, more charitably tomorrow. Finally, we commit to going onward, to continuing the work of realizing God's dream for our world, even in all its challenge.

The Examen is a versatile prayer: There are versions to help us ferret out racism, recognize the injustices of a changing climate, assess our responsibilities as citizens of particular countries, and so on. But regardless of how the Examen manifests itself, there is a common through line of thanksgiving. We *always* begin in gratitude.

I found this a little odd. When I interviewed the Jesuit priest and acclaimed spiritual writer Mark Thibodeaux about the Examen, I asked him if it was appropriate or perhaps a little offensive to insist on beginning with gratitude when our prayer necessarily demands that we look at war, violence, ecological degradation, and a host of other injustices. How can we start by saying thanks? What are we saying thank you *for*?

Father Thibodeaux nodded his head. He understood what I was getting at. "But if we begin instead by looking solely at the many problems of our world," he said, "we narrow our gaze. We go down a rabbit hole of despair. We focus on what we lack."[11]

Instead, he insisted, if we begin in gratitude, we begin with giftedness. We expand our imagination, lift the horizon of what's possible. We realize that we are beloved, even against a backdrop of such pain and darkness. We are *gift* and *gifted*. In embracing this truth, that we have the ability to meet this moment, we begin to do exactly that. We respond in creativity, charity, and hope—even against impossible odds. By reframing our stories—even our past day—through the lens of grace and giftedness and gratitude, we look not for where things have gone wrong but for how we have been given an opportunity to set them right.

This is not fast work; this is a life's slow journey. One step forward, in the company of others. But it is a journey we can undertake if we train our eyes on the gift we uniquely are to the world.

How might we engage this Spirit of giftedness in our own quest for inner peace? How might we ask the Spirit of gift to reframe our understanding of self so as to make us more able to embrace our unique *magis* and meet this moment as we find it?

A Spiritual Exercise for Peace Work

Opening Prayer

Pray for the grace to embrace your identity as God's beloved—and to see each and every person you encounter as God sees them.

Prayer Text

Then Jesus came from Galilee to John at the Jordan to be baptized by him. John tried to prevent him, saying, "I need to be baptized by you, and yet you are coming to me?" Jesus said to him in reply, "Allow it now, for thus it is fitting for us to fulfill all righteousness." Then he allowed him. After Jesus was baptized, he came up from the water and behold, the heavens were opened [for him], and he saw the Spirit of God descending like a dove [and] coming upon him. And a voice came from the heavens, saying, "This is my beloved Son, with whom I am well pleased."

Matthew 3:13–17

Reflection Exercises

- At first, John is reluctant to baptize Jesus. He couldn't have known that, in fact, he was standing in the way of Jesus hearing those words, "You are my beloved." When have we stood in the way of another's experience of belovedness? When have we stood in our *own* way? How did this cost us and others inner peace?
- Place yourself in the scene. Imagine you are being baptized by John. What do you feel, smell, see? How does the coldness and

darkness of the water affect you? When you come back up for air, what is your first thought? Then, the voice of God speaks directly to you—what does it mean to be God's beloved?

Conversation

- Have you ever thought of yourself as beloved? How does this essential identity—the beloved of God—change how you see your life story? In conversation with God or with a neighbor, review a key moment from your past that your belovedness reframes.

Journal

- Spend time praying with the Examen. Remember the five steps: (1) begin in gratitude; (2) ask the Spirit to shed light on your day; (3) carefully review the day's events; (4) look clearly at where mistakes were made; (5) commit to continue drawing nearer to God tomorrow. As you write down your reflections, what do you see? How has the Spirit been speaking throughout your day?

CHAPTER 3

Seeing Suffering, Dreaming Peace

One of the assigned texts in a course I took my first year of college was the book of Job. It wasn't a theology course, though one of the professors was a theologian. The other was a philosopher. The course was an interdisciplinary inquiry called "Ideas That Shaped the West." The Judeo-Christian concept of God—and in particular, a God who "allows" suffering—certainly qualified as one of those ideas.

I had never spent much time with the story of Job, so the two class meetings where the book took center stage were revelatory. We were going to delve into the nature of suffering, the *why* of it all. Naive as I was, I thought we were going to walk out of class that Thursday with a satisfying answer to the perennial conundrum of why bad things happen to good people.

The book of Job, rather than giving an answer to the question of suffering, simply puts the spotlight *on* suffering. Job, a "blameless and upright" individual by God's own admission (Job 2:3), suddenly finds himself put to a seemingly frivolous test. Will he, under severe pressure, hardship, and the evil and attentive eye of Satan himself, curse God? Or will he remain steadfast in his faithfulness? Seemingly curious to learn the outcome, God gives Job over to Satan with only one instruction: "He is in your power; only spare his life" (2:6).

Satan has at it. Job suddenly loses his money and resources, his children, and his health. He quickly shifts from prosperity to misery. Job is understandably unhappy, but what does his story tell us about God and violence and suffering?

This chapter is not an exercise in theodicy; I will not try to answer the question of why God permits evil. It's enough simply to know that suffering exists, just one of the many results of a lack of peace. But I do think that the book of Job—as well as the general theme of lamentation present throughout Scripture—proves illustrative to how we find peace within ourselves and within our world. Simply recognizing ourselves as the beloved of God does not mean we avoid suffering, but ours is a God to whom we can and should cry out, a God who cries with us. In this chapter we will wrestle with the interwoven mystery of suffering and peace.

The Spiritual Exercises of Ignatius of Loyola begin in a place such as this: The First Week invites us to look plainly at the evils in our world, at the sin and suffering from which God desires to free us. Thus, this chapter will also be an exercise in taking a long, hard look at the obstacles in our lives that prevent peace and produce pain.

Evil on (the) Job

The book of Job is a series of monologues and dialogues—Job crying aloud, trying to make sense of his fall from grace; three of his friends trying to cheer him up; and God finally answering. Job laments:

> For to me sighing comes more readily than food;
>   my groans well forth like water.
> For what I feared overtakes me;
>   what I dreaded comes upon me.
> I have no peace nor ease;
>   I have no rest, for trouble has come! (Job 3:24–26)

This sentiment is certainly something many of us have felt. A crying out to God from the lowest of lows, our own drowning in a cascade of sorrow and suffering. This is the kind of pain you feel in your very soul.

Job's friends respond, and quite unhelpfully: "Happy the one whom God reproves!" (Job 5:17). Really? Happy? They continue:

> The Almighty's discipline do not reject.
> For he wounds, but he binds up;
>   he strikes, but his hands give healing.
> Out of six troubles he will deliver you,
>   and at the seventh no evil shall touch you.
>   In famine he will deliver you from death,
>   and in war from the power of the sword;
> From the scourge of the tongue you shall be hidden,
>   and you shall not fear approaching ruin.
>   (Job 5:17–21)

On and on it goes until Job finally exclaims, "Let the Almighty answer me! Let my accuser write out his indictment!" (31:35).

In short, Job is really suffering, and his friends are offering platitudes: *Everything happens for a reason. God never gives us more than we can bear. What doesn't kill you makes you stronger.*

We've all been there—on both sides of the equation. We've found ourselves awash in hardship. The death of a loved one.

Financial burdens. Rocky relationships. An uncertain future. Addiction and violence and terror. While we may know that God is at work—somehow, somewhere—platitudes like those of Job's friends are rarely useful in the moment. Our head and our heart are not singing from the same songbook.

Such platitudes not only fall short, they often risk offending: What about victims of war, natural disaster, addiction, and so much else? In those cases, it appears God *did* give them more than they could bear. Job's friends speak of healing hands and bound wounds and deliverance from violence and famine, but a cursory glance at present-day headlines seems to show these positive outcomes to be woefully lacking.

Yet when we find ourselves on the other side, observing suffering from a safe distance, what can we really offer? We want to *respond*. We want to *fix*. We want to *do*. But too often, all we can do is be present to that suffering. There are no words. There are often no answers.

There is only us and our God who, though we may not understand God's answers, does hear our heartfelt cry. Just as important, God desires that we express our anger and pain and sorrow.

Holy Tears

How do I know that God desires us to express our pain rather than bottle it up? Three words: "And Jesus wept" (John 11:35).

Jesus has returned to Bethany to find that his friend Lazarus has died. Martha and Mary, Lazarus's sisters and Jesus's friends, are understandably distraught and confused about why the Son of God, notorious miracle worker and healer of the sick, couldn't have arrived just a *tad* earlier to, you know, work a miracle and heal his friend. As he makes his way to the tomb, Jesus is full of, if not platitudes, then at the very least what seem to be unhelpful words of not-quite comfort: "I am glad for you that I was not there, that you may believe. . . . Your brother will rise. . . . Whoever believes in me, even if he dies, will live" (John 11:15, 23, 25).

Then Jesus sees the suffering firsthand. Mary, Lazarus's sister, is weeping. Others in the community are weeping. Jesus seems at a loss for words. A man is dead, and even in the presence of the Christ, sorrow is still raw and real.

Then Jesus himself breaks down. *And Jesus wept.*

I'm always struck by that simple line, this admission that our own God is so moved by suffering that the only response possible is one of tears and emotion. It's worth remembering: We're made in the image and likeness of this very God. We, like Jesus, are rightly overcome by the sorrow of our world. We, like Jesus, rightly cry out.

We are made in the image and likeness of a God who weeps.

A Long, Loving Look

A pillar of Ignatian spirituality is the radical notion that we are called to live as contemplatives in action. One of Ignatius's earliest companions—the Jesuit priest Jerome Nadal—coined the expression "contemplatives in action" as a way to differentiate Jesuit life *in the world* from the more typical religious life of the time, namely, *in the monastery.* This idea of living as a contemplative in action is arguably even more relevant and vital to us today. Cultivating a disposition of contemplation in action can help us truly see the suffering of others and be moved so much by what we encounter that we weep in the image and likeness of our God. In this way, we prepare our hearts for meaningful accompaniment and action.

What does it mean to live as a contemplative in action? My favorite definition comes from Jesuit Walter Burghardt. He challenges us to see contemplation as a *long, loving look at the real.* "The *real,* reality, is not reducible to some far-off abstract, intangible God-in-the-sky. Reality is living, pulsing people; reality is fire and ice," he writes. "This real I *look* at. I do not analyze or argue it, describe or define it; I am one with it. I do not move around it; I enter into it . . . to 'look' wholly means that my whole person reacts." Burghardt invites us to settle into this loving look; it necessarily takes time, and that time might make us uncomfortable. "To contemplate is to rest—to rest in the real. Not lifelessly or languidly, not sluggishly or inertly. My entire being is alive, incredibly responsive, vibrating to every throb of the real."[1]

In short, we don't shy away from the real pain so pervasive in our world. We don't wall ourselves off from others. We, like Jesus, go to encounter suffering and—even if we've been offering platitudes and euphemisms and pretty words all along—allow ourselves to be struck silent by what we find. "From such contemplation comes communion," writes Burghardt. "I mean the discovery of the Holy in deep, thoughtful encounters—with God's creation, with God's people, with God's self—where love is proven by sacrifice, the wild exchange of all for another, for the Other."[2] Contemplation allows us to settle into reality—our own reality, the reality of others—and develop an understanding of and empathy for experiences that may vary dramatically from our own. This is a key element of the First Week of the Exercises.

We need each other, and I don't just mean for a shoulder to lean on. If we are to build peace, to act on the demands of peace in our lives and our world, we need to do it together, hand in hand. And we need to build from a common understanding of reality. We need to truly see one another's suffering.

Jesus in the Garden

There is consolation in what might seem an unusual place within Scripture: Jesus's agony in the garden of Gethsemane.

The consolation isn't because the scene itself is a cheerful one. Rather, we see Jesus, God Incarnate, grapple with his own suffering. And he doesn't do so quietly. He doesn't grin and bear it. He doesn't shrug it off and say, "I guess everything happens for a reason."

No—he goes directly to God in lament.

"Father, if you are willing, take this cup away from me," Jesus says. "Still, not my will but yours be done" (Luke 22:42). We may read these words and forget to place ourselves in the scene, but Ignatius of Loyola himself draws our attention to a significant, troubling detail. In his Spiritual Exercises he writes, "Then Jesus began his prayer, and his sweat became as drops of blood. Three times he prayed to his father."[3] Luke 22:44 says, "He was in such agony and he prayed so fervently that his sweat became like drops of blood falling on the ground."

We can imagine Jesus shivering, his body shaking uncontrollably at the very thought of what was to come. He's feverish, anxious, physically ill. And he feels so alone—despite the fact that his friends wait for him not so far away. From this place of pain, Jesus—the beloved of God—reaches out to that same God.

Have we experienced such pain? Have we accompanied another in such a moment?

"I am troubled now," Jesus prays. "Yet what should I say? 'Father, save me from this hour'? But it was for this purpose that I came to this hour. Father, glorify your name." This time, in John's telling, God answers, "I have glorified it and will glorify it again" (John 12:27–28).

Even here, in this moment of intense suffering, Jesus points us to a universal truth: We still bring our full selves to the moment. *It was for this purpose that I came to this hour.* What does this tell us? That our own *magis* is still necessarily at work, even here, even now. There are still actions to be taken that bring us closer to that end for which we have been made.

There is something here, even in the suffering, that *only* we can uniquely accomplish.

The will of God is not some abstract thing forced upon us; it is a harmonious chord that strikes our very soul. We don't need to "accept" God's will begrudgingly as something happening to us. We live God's will through that constant unfolding of our own unique vocation. The will of God and our own deepest desire are two overlapping circles on the Venn diagram of our lives. Even in moments of suffering.

We have to settle into the realness of this moment. For ourselves, yes, but we also must recognize and accompany each person who finds themselves in such a situation—and there are many. In each of these moments, too, is a unique experience of God, some essential piece of *magis*, God's will unfolding. What's true for us is true for each and every person. We go to God together; we need one another.

As we do so, as we recognize that *we're still here* and we're still *us*, God is glorified. God, who is manifested in an entirely unique way through our very selves.

Just Dance

Suffering is awful. We don't seek it out, and we definitely don't look from afar at the suffering of others and say, "Hey, good for you! Don't forget to look for God! Things are going to turn out great!"

Still, I find myself returning to a particularly poignant evening I spent in the Jesuit Center in Amman, Jordan. I was there to gather the stories of refugees who had been forced to flee their homes, who witnessed friends and family members die in the process. I was there to film and photograph and write, so as to bring the plight of these young women and men to our audience in the United States and Canada. In many ways, I was there to tell the story of suffering.

This, of course, was the wrong way to approach the experience. *Here comes the American, ready to receive your sad stories and share them with the world!* And I was quickly put in my place.

Naturally, the story of suffering was unavoidable. These young people came from war-torn communities in Sudan and Iraq and Somalia and elsewhere. But the essential piece of their stories wasn't the suffering—though it was inevitable. The essential piece was what came next.

What came next was bound up in their own vocations, their own passions and desires and hopes. Their *magis*.

I met one young man who we will call Amani.[4] Amani had fled Sudan due to war. He arrived at the Jesuit Center in Amman like so many others, seeking safety and unsure of what came next. He enrolled in an English language program and began to meet other members of the community.

By his own admission, Amani arrived hating people of Arabic background, hating White people, and hating people of other religions. "I was very lonely," he told me. He sat in front of my camera, one of dozens of young people who spoke with me that night. "I used to hate everything. I was something different." He was simply drawing from his own experience in Sudan. Who could blame him? Given the horrors of war, violence, death, and destruction, his anger was understandable.

It would seem that God was *not* willing to take that cup away from Amani. What should I say in response—"I guess it made you stronger"? Of course not.

But then he went on. I had been prodded by one of the Jesuits there to ask him about a dance class he taught for other members of the community—refugees like him, from all over the world.

"I came to know people," he said. "I didn't want to learn dance and stuff. I wanted to change my mood and change my routine." As it turned out, Amani was—*is*—a great dancer.

"When you dance with a group of people, you can just see yourself, like you're in a party. It's very good to dance with people of different nationalities." What about the distrust and hatred he had toward other people, people of different backgrounds and faiths? "We just see ourselves as human beings."

Years have passed, but I still think about Amani's story. He's not a professional dancer; he didn't leave Sudan hoping for a career in a dance troupe. But he arrived in Jordan, carrying burdens I'll never fully understand, and gave of himself. He showed up with what he had. He challenged himself to step out of his comfort zone and, more so, out of and away from what he believed about the world. In doing so, he discovered something about himself. Something he didn't even know existed.

I attended one of his dance classes and filmed it. There were a couple dozen people in an upper room at the Jesuit Center just having a good time. Building something together. Enjoying one another's company.

A glimmer of peace came to Amani in that unlooked-for skillset. And he leaned in; he shared it with others. That peace glimmered and sparkled, and something grew.

A Fairy-Tale Ending

What I remember most about the book of Job from that college course I took was the deep skepticism I left with that Thursday afternoon. My professors had raised their eyebrows at the ending of Job's story. Here is a book-length tale about a guy God tests for little discernible reason. He suffers and struggles and cries out. His friends are no help. God's answer is distant and, seemingly, unhelpful: "Would you refuse to acknowledge my right? Would you condemn me that you may be justified? Have you an arm like that of God, or can you thunder with a voice like his? . . . Everything under the heavens is mine" (Job 40:8–9; 41:3).

In short: I'm God; you're not. Deal with it.

Job finally throws up his hands, defeated: "I have spoken but did not understand; things too marvelous for me, which I did not know" (Job 42:3).

It's not a satisfying answer to the mystery of suffering, but it is likely one we can all relate to. It's perhaps one we feel in our guts—*Oh. Things really are terrible, and there's no reason that I'll ever fully understand to justify any of it, and I just muddle on from one hardship to the next.*

It's a tough lesson to swallow, but look out at the world: Is it so hard to see the confusion and chaos that suffering brings? I don't know what conflicts might be occurring now in your life as you're reading these words, but I know some that are occurring while I write them: Children are killed in their sleep as bombs fall on civilians going about their daily lives.

Then Job's story takes a sudden and unexpected turn. God changes Job's fortunes, dismisses his friends, and takes dramatic action. "The LORD also restored the prosperity of Job, after he had prayed for his friends; the LORD even gave to Job twice as much as he had before" (Job 42:10).

Huh? Just as we're about to nod sadly and say, yes, indeed the world is unfair, we arrive at a fairy-tale ending? That was the bit that gave my professors pause. To be honest, I paused too. The ending feels too much like, "Just grin and bear it—it'll all work out." That's just not everyone's experience. Maybe not even most people's experience. How many people die each day without ever having their suffering relieved or their lives restored?

The thing about war—any violence, really—is that it takes only one party to start it. Peace, on the other hand, requires every party to be involved. There are no shortcuts, no sudden bouts of peace. It is built and maintained slowly, over time, and with very few fairies.

That's why taking a long, loving look at the real is so important. We must sink into the experiences of others so that we can *together* build and sustain that peace. We must dance with one another. We must recognize one another as beloved with some essential piece of the *magis* to offer the world. We must come together to get to know one another if we want a shot at our fairy-tale endings becoming reality.

Here's the thing about fairy-tale endings. "The consolation of fairy-stories, the joy of the happy ending . . . is not essentially 'escapist,'" writes J. R. R. Tolkien. "It does not deny the existence of . . . sorrow or failure: the possibility of these is necessary to the joy of deliverance; it denies universal final defeat and in so far is *evangelium*, giving a fleeting glimpse of Joy, Joy beyond the walls of the world, poignant as grief."[5]

The so-called fairy-tale ending in the book of Job points us beyond ourselves, beyond our individual lives and suffering. It glimmers with possibility, with the whispered promise that, indeed, there is hope for peace and hope for redemption. That, although there is so much pain and agony in our world and although the cup is rarely taken from us, we still muddle onward toward God's dream. "The Evangelium has not abrogated legends; it has hallowed them, especially the 'happy ending,'" Tolkien writes. "The Christian has still to work, with mind as well as body, to suffer, hope and die; but [they] may now perceive that all [their] bents and faculties have a purpose, which can be redeemed."[6]

No platitudes. No euphemisms. Simply at times the uncomfortable truth that, as we struggle for peace within ourselves and our world, we struggle also to manifest something unique about ourselves that can meet the needs of this moment in all its lamentation and joy and wonder.

To quote the novelist Neil Gaiman, who, in the opening pages of his own dark fairy-tale *Coraline*, paraphrases G. K. Chesterton, "Fairy tales are more than true: not because they tell us that dragons exist, but because they tell us that dragons can be beaten."[7]

Our God is a not a god who plays frivolous games with our lives. Rather, our God invites us to look clearly at the evils in our world—and then beyond them to God's great dream of justice, compassion, and peace. The work of peace necessarily takes us through suffering. We can only emerge on the other side if we continue to dream that peace is possible.

A Spiritual Exercise for Peace Work

Opening Prayer

Pray for the grace to truly see suffering so as to more clearly see what peace requires.

Prayer Text

After this, Job opened his mouth and cursed his day. Job spoke out and said:

> Perish the day on which I was born,
>   the night when they said, "The child is a boy!"
> May that day be darkness:
>   may God above not care for it,
>   may light not shine upon it!
> May darkness and gloom claim it,
>   clouds settle upon it,
>   blackness of day affright it!
> May obscurity seize that night;
>   may it not be counted among the days of the year,
>   nor enter into the number of the months!
> May that night be barren;
>   let no joyful outcry greet it!
> Let them curse it who curse the Sea,
>   those skilled at disturbing Leviathan!

May the stars of its twilight be darkened;
    may it look for daylight, but have none,
    nor gaze on the eyes of the dawn,
Because it did not keep shut the doors of the womb
    to shield my eyes from trouble!

Job 3:1–10

Reflection Exercises

- Read Job's lament slowly, letting each turn of phrase settle into your soul. What do you feel? What do you feel *for Job*? Do these feelings stir you to act? Or are you able to simply sit with these words and the one who speaks them?
- As you let Job's words wash over you, what insights do you get into the needs of peace? How does inner peace affect peace within communities? If Job was in your community, what would you say?

Conversation

- Spend time meditating on Jesus's words to God: "My Father, if it is possible, let this cup pass from me; yet, not as I will, but as you will" (Matt. 26:39). Think about whether you are currently carrying a particularly full cup. What does God say to you about it?

Journal

- Return to Job's lament. Can you imagine similar words being cried aloud by people today? Who? Why? Have you felt these words in your own soul? Spend time describing the situation that leads to words and feelings such as Job's. Where is there a lack of peace? How might deeper understanding of one another's suffering birth new ways of building peace?

CHAPTER 4

Cannonballs, Peace, and the Ignatian Imagination

The early 1990s saw devastation befall the people of Bosnia and Herzegovina. The Soviet Union crumbled, Yugoslavia was dissolved, and suddenly the ethnonationalistic identities of the Serbs, Bosniaks, and Croats that had been suppressed for decades erupted into bloody conflict throughout the Balkans. The newly independent country of Bosnia and Herzegovina was caught in the middle, literally stuck between Serbia and Croatia. Sarajevo, the capital of Bosnia and Herzegovina, had hosted the Winter Olympics in 1984; eight years later, it was under a siege that would last four brutal years.

I was seven years old when the Dayton Accords were signed, devising a fragile end to the conflict through a three-way power-sharing agreement among the Serbs, Bosniaks, and Croats. The year was 1995, and I was preoccupied with moving from California to Pennsylvania, starting a new school, making new friends, and discovering a new home. The conflict didn't register in my mind. Why would it? I was a kid and a long way from the Balkan Peninsula.

Some twenty years later, though, I stood in the streets of Sarajevo. I made a somber pilgrimage to the place where Archduke Franz Ferdinand was assassinated, prompting the events of World War I. I met with leaders of the three major religious communities—Roman Catholic, Orthodox, and Muslim—who also represented the three corresponding ethnic groups: Croat, Serb, and Bosniak, respectively. I heard stories from peacebuilders, professionals who made it their business to hold together the very shaky foundation upon which the entire society was built. I was part of a delegation from Catholic Relief Services— the international humanitarian response and development agency of the US Catholic Church—and we were visiting and learning from our colleagues and partners.

But what struck me time and again was that peace was present at all. Not so much that the society was functioning— though that, too, was a minor miracle—but that the people I met were able to press on with their daily lives. The brutal fact that the bloody, deadly, and cruel conflict was very much in living memory of each individual I encountered bowled me over. Every person I met who was my age or older had lived through it and had a story to tell about their own desperate acts of survival. Everyone had been affected. Everyone had faced the unimaginable. Neighbors had turned on one another. With each passing conversation, I became more amazed and humbled.

The people of Bosnia and Herzegovina had lived through tragedy but pressed on all the same. The scars were still raw and exposed. These were resilient people. But they are hardly the only ones to have lived through such suffering. I think of the people of Rwanda and Sudan; communities all across the Middle East; the families I met in Vietnam. On and on the list could go. The determination of individuals to move forward in the wake of massive human suffering and evil inspires awe in me. Standing there in Sarajevo only reinforced that assessment. In this chapter, I want to explore the human resolve to take stock and carry on despite profound suffering. There is a somewhat flippant term in the Ignatian tradition that points to the hinge experience of tragedy and hardship—we call it a cannonball moment, for reasons I'll soon explain. We're knocked off our feet, turned around entirely, stripped down and kicked out, and made to look anew at our lives and our place therein.

We'll talk about cannonball moments and put them into context, but for our own reflection on peace and spirituality, the importance of a cannonball moment isn't the moment itself; it's what we do in the aftermath. How we allow our imagination to unfold—or not. How we allow seeds of peace to be planted in the upturned soil of our lives. How we muddle onward toward hoped-for peace within ourselves and within our communities.

An Auspicious Refusal

The term *cannonball moment* is exactly what it sounds like, but let me give some backstory.

In 1491, during the reign of King Ferdinand and Queen Isabella, Ignatius of Loyola was born in the Basque region of Spain to a family of some nobility. He was baptized Iñigo; it wouldn't be until sometime between 1535 and 1540 that he began to sign his name "Ignatius." Iñigo's early life was marked by early tragedy; both his mother and father died while he was still young. As a result, he was sent to live with a relative at court—the royal treasurer. Here he developed a love of fighting, chasing women, gambling, and feeding his growing ego.[1]

For young Iñigo, success in life was measured by military prowess. "Up to the age of twenty-six, he was a man given to the vanities of the world; and what he enjoyed most was warlike sport, with a great and foolish desire to win fame," he said of himself.[2] And so, in 1521 at the Battle of Pamplona, when the superior French fighting force offered to accept the surrender of the outmaneuvered Spanish battalion, Iñigo refused. He writes of his own actions in his autobiography (dictated in the third person): "And so . . . when all were of the view that they should surrender, with their lives safeguarded—for they saw clearly that they could not offer resistance—he [Iñigo] gave so many reasons to the commander that he actually persuaded him to resist, even against this view of all the officers, who drew courage from his spirit and determination."[3] Unfortunately, they were indeed outnumbered. As a result, Iñigo got a cannonball to the legs. The battle was lost, and a vast number of Iñigo's fellow soldiers lay dead.

Iñigo's cannonball moment demanded that he reimagine what his life would be. The injured soldier was ferried home to the family castle at Loyola. Despite having his legs broken and reset multiple times, he would forever walk with a limp—an unthinkable attribute for a man dreaming of a life at court. Eleven months elapsed as Iñigo recovered in his bed. While there, he yearned for battle and the romance of his old life. He daydreamed about his courtly pursuits, but he found that such memories left him feeling dry, empty, and restless.

Magdalena, his sister-in-law and the one entrusted with his care during his recovery, claimed there were only two books available to Iñigo in the castle. So when the young man asked for stories of knights and romance, he instead received a book on the life of the saints and a book on the life of Christ. Begrudgingly, he read them. To his surprise, he discovered that his imagination ran wild, fueled by these sacred stories. They left him feeling energized and with an invitation: Could he, too, lead such a life? In the weeks, months, and years that followed, Ignatius put down his sword and picked up the staff of a pilgrim.

We all experience cannonball moments. We have all had our lives turned upside down, our dreams dashed, our expectations for who and what we might become cast to the side. Cannonball moments need not be bloody, violent affairs. The death of a loved one, the loss of a job, an unexpected move, or a setback for a child are all cannonball moments. Certainly, as you reflect on your own life, a moment or several come to your mind. How did these moments reset the trajectory of your story?

For the people of Bosnia and Herzegovina, for the families of Iñigo's fellow soldiers, and for so many communities around the world, cannonball moments *are* bloody, violent affairs. After all, the cannonball itself is a tool of war designed to inflict suffering and devastation.

My friend Robert McChesney, a Jesuit priest, has spent much of his life accompanying folks who have experienced trauma: refugees, veterans of war, victims of abuse, and others. I met Rob when I visited the Jesuit Center in Amman, Jordan. He was providing spiritual direction to many members of the community and serving as a chaplain for Jesuit Refugee Service. When I returned to the United States, I invited Rob to join me on the podcast I cohost to talk about his work, what he had learned, and what he was thinking about as he prepared to end his time in Jordan.[4]

We spent a great deal of time talking about cannonball moments. I assumed Rob was an expert on cannonball moments because of his work; after all, traumatic experiences often force us to reassess who we are and where we're going. But Rob was uncomfortable with the expression—and for good reason. It's easy to romanticize a cannonball moment. It's also grossly disrespectful, patronizing, and dangerous.

"How would you like it if someone called it a 'shrapnel' moment?" Rob asked. Reflecting back on comments he'd heard from people he had worked with in the veterans' community, he explained that this was like celebrating women and men getting weapons of war trapped in their bodies. There's nothing innately good about that.[5]

Rob and I have had this conversation time and time again. It's an important one because in the Ignatian tradition we *do* celebrate cannonball moments. We hold them up as something important—and they are. But what we too often forget about Ignatius's *own* cannonball moment is that the moment itself was nothing but tragic. It wasn't the pain and suffering that turned Ignatius into a saint; he didn't emerge from Pamplona holier, with some existential insight, simply for having been injured. It was the period of recovery afterward that changed him, the time of prayer and reflection and imagination.

When we speak of cannonball moments, we must be clear that we are not glorifying the violence, the trauma, the suffering. Rather, we are pointing to the opportunity—tragic as it may be—that the moment represents. Cannonball moments put us at hinge points in our lives, when the door of our story can swing one way or another, and we must choose which direction to walk. These are not onetime decisions; building peace within ourselves and our communities never is. But in the time of healing and reflection that follows, we set ourselves upon a path. Will that path be one that solidifies the status quo of our lives, or one that dares to dream of something new?

The Moral Imagination

We've already reflected on the importance of the imagination within Ignatian spirituality. It is through our own creative imagining that we settle into scenes of Scripture, as Ignatius invites us to do throughout the Spiritual Exercises. We use our imagination to compose the scenes of Scripture, to engage our senses as we walk with Christ and his disciples and the many characters of the Gospel stories. This is a uniquely Ignatian way to approach a sacred text.

But this is not the only way Ignatian spirituality invites us to use our imagination. Return to the scene of Ignatius lying on his bed after losing his mobility and many of his friends. Convalescing in his home at Loyola, he battles depression, loneliness, and failure. He has nothing *but* his imagination, and he uses it to weigh his potential futures. He tries to conjure up the chivalric scenes that had given him such comfort and purpose, to little avail. It's only when he imagines his life unfolding in a new way, inspired by the life and legacy of Christ and the saints, that he finds solace. He imagines using his chivalric skills for the good of God's people rather than for some earthly ruler.

From the devastation of the cannonball strikes and through the long, tortuous period of healing, Ignatius engages his imagination so he can choose which path to take—and he puts his old ways of living behind him. In his prayer, in his reflection, he asks, "What might my life yet be?" This, too, is engaging the imagination in the Ignatian tradition.

What does this have to do with peace? Everything. From a life riddled by violence, from a moment of arrogance and bloodshed, Ignatius sets off on a road of peace by way of the imagination. It is a personal peace, as Ignatius begins to discover his own *magis* and recognize the unique unfolding of his own vocation, but it is also communal. This new way of life both *rejects* the way of violence that had so dominated Ignatius's life and *lays the foundation* for a community built on justice, compassion, and mercy—the Society of Jesus in particular, and all of us who engage with the Ignatian tradition in general.

The renowned peacebuilder John Paul Lederach uses a term that's apt to our reflections here: the moral imagination. He defines it "as the capacity to imagine something rooted in the challenges of the real world yet capable of giving birth to that which does not yet exist."[6] We might hear in these words the challenge of being contemplatives in action: We take a long, loving look at the real. From that place, we act. Again and again, when grappling with overwhelming devastation, we realize that the old ways aren't good enough. Our actions must reveal something *new*, and that new must first be imagined into being.

"In reference to peacebuilding," Lederach continues, "this is the capacity to imagine and generate constructive responses and initiatives that, while rooted in the day-to-day challenges of violence, transcend and ultimately break the grips of those destructive patterns and cycles."[7] We never shy away from the truth of the moment: our pain, that of others, the damage done to our communities and creation. We do not glorify a cannonball moment, as Father McChesney reminds us, but we do look at it squarely and allow ourselves to be affected by it. Then we begin the slow, circuitous work of imagining a new way forward, of allowing the hinge moment to open up a new chapter in our story.

"Turning points are moments pregnant with new life, which rise from what appear to be the barren grounds of destructive violence and relationships," Lederach writes. "However, such pregnant moments do not emerge through the rote application of a technique or a recipe. They must be explored and understood in the context of something that approximates the artistic process, imbued as it is with creativity, skill, serendipity and craftsmanship."[8] We must open ourselves up to the Spirit of Creativity at work in our lives. We must allow ourselves to be surprised by what God desires to write with our unique imaginations.

Turning the Status Quo Upside Down

There's a troubling fact about Ignatius's cannonball moment that I often find myself considering: It was completely unnecessary. It didn't need to happen! The young Iñigo's pride was the only reason the Spanish forces didn't surrender. Iñigo refused such perceived failure and instead insisted on continuing the fight. Continuing to do things the way they'd always been done despite all the evidence at hand. Continuing to uphold a status quo that was so clearly broken: Violence begets violence begets violence.

At the microlevel, the pride that insisted on maintaining a failing status quo resulted in the destruction of both: Ignatius was humbled and forced to surrender his sword. More accurately, he found himself with the opportunity to choose. Would he recognize the evil his pride had unleashed and work against it? Would he lay down his sword and set off on a new way of life? Would he break the cycle of violence that had so entangled his story?

Of course, if he had accepted the French terms of surrender, would we be reflecting on Ignatius at all? Would we have a thing called Ignatian spirituality or the Spiritual Exercises? Ignatius may have continued on as a soldier and man about court, and nothing more. The suffering and pain represented by the cannonball moment is not itself a good thing, yet still we see the good that can result. But it all comes down to our choices, how we grapple with the broken pieces of reality around us.

Joseph Campbell, the great scholar of world myths and religions, writes about the hero's journey. There is a moment—an instigating factor, a catalyst—when the hero is given the opportunity to leave the status quo of their old life and embark on the road to adventure. But the protagonist must respond to the call of adventure. Luke Skywalker could have stayed on Tatooine. Dorothy could have given up on Toto. Moses could have ignored the burning bush. Ignatius could have limped back to his life at court, making the best of a bad situation. The call of adventure is not something we have to respond to; we can ignore it. "The myths and folktales of the whole world make clear that the refusal is essentially a refusal to give up what one takes to be one's own interest," writes Campbell.[9] So when we do reject the call, we often suffer in the status quo world we continue to inhabit, a world that so often means violence, suffering, and death. We reject the opportunity to imagine something new.

For us and our desire to build peace, that simply is not an option. We step out of the status quo and into the unknown.

In her wonderful book on fiction writing, *Save the Cat! Writes a Novel: The Last Book on Novel Writing You'll Ever Need*, Jessica Brody gives a name to the place in which we now find ourselves: Act 2, the upside-down world. The status quo has been turned on its head and everything is different. We find ourselves imagining what life would be like as a Jedi knight or living in the Land of Oz or standing up to the Pharaoh or perhaps even becoming a mystic saint. We *need* to engage our imagination, though, because everything is necessarily new.

To help us along the way, we meet a mentor character, a guide. Glinda the Good Witch or Gandalf the Grey or Obi-Wan Kenobi or our fairy godmother. Brody says there are only two important criteria about these characters: First, "they must in some way represent the upside-down Act 2 world," and second, "they must in some way help guide the hero toward their life lesson or theme. The first criterion means that the hero could never have met or noticed this character in Act 1. It was only because of the Catalyst and subsequent Break Into 2 that this . . . character fully came into the hero's life."[10]

Now, you may say, "Eric, why are you quoting books on fiction writing? This is supposed to be about peace and spirituality." Of course, you are right. But Brody, like Campbell, is reflecting on good storytelling technique, and good storytelling technique is good because it is grounded in stories that are *true*. Stories like ours, yours and mine. Brody is pointing to something quite profound that is essential for our own lives: We too often look for our own mentor figures in individuals we find in our status quo world. And these people, good-hearted as they may be, can't help us imagine a new way of being if they, too, are bound to the old.

We cannot transcend violence and suffering and war and conflict if we keep looking to those who profit and prosper from the maintenance of this way of life. To properly engage our moral imagination, we must answer the call to adventure and step beyond the status quo that our own cannonball moments have revealed—and broken.

For Ignatius, that mentor figure from the upside-down world was quite simply Jesus Christ. It was an encounter with Jesus in prayer and reflection that got Ignatius out of bed and headed in a new direction. This life-changing encounter is why Ignatius gives prominence in the Spiritual Exercises to an essential meditation called the Call of Christ the King, or the Kingdom Meditation.

Yes—right there in the Spiritual Exercises is a call to step into the upside-down world and discover adventure.

Christ Beckons

The Call of Christ the King, or the Kingdom Meditation, is a key moment in the Spiritual Exercises, bridging the first and second weeks. In the First Week, as we've been discovering in these last two chapters, the retreatant awakens to sin, disorder, and violence in their personal lives and their world, as well as the interconnection among the three. Rather than allowing us to dwell in shame or guilt, the Call of Christ is a reminder that God does not condemn but invites. God wants us to be up and about the business of realizing God's dream for the world.

And so, Christ beckons to us to *collaborate* in the Christ project: the universal reordering of relationships, the healing of the cosmos and one another, the realization of God's vision for creation here, now while also always pointing to what lies beyond. What's more, Christ *desires to work with us*, to join us in the hard, grueling but joy-filled work. Christ is not a leader who directs from afar; rather, he reflects our God who dwells intimately in our very selves. Our response, then, is to be people *with* and not merely *for* others, as Jesus is.

As the Second Week of the Exercises unfolds, we see this servant leader—Jesus Christ—at work, ministering to the sick, the wounded, the hurting, the forgotten, and we join in this effort. While this meditation—the Call of Christ—and its context are unique to the Exercises, the heart of the meditation—that is, our response to Christ in our lives—is at the center of the Christian life. This meditation is both uniquely Ignatian and universally Christian.

Christ invites each of us along the path of our own unique vocation. There are as many vocational journeys, as many responses to Christ's call, as there are people in this world. Each of us discovers and discerns that call in any number of different ways. Where is Christ speaking to you? Where is Christ calling you *today*? How—through *whom*—do you hear that call? How do you respond? And *why*?

Ultimately, these questions lead us to the three foundational questions Ignatius wants us to keep always at the forefront of our minds: *What have I done for Christ? What am I doing for Christ? What ought I do for Christ?*

These are the words Ignatius imagines Christ speaking to each of us in the Kingdom Meditation: "It is my will to conquer the whole world and all my enemies, and thus to enter into the glory of my Father. Therefore, whoever wishes to join me in this enterprise must be willing to labor with me, that by following me in suffering, he may follow me in glory."[11] Ignatius finishes by saying, "Consider that all persons who have judgment and reason will offer themselves entirely for this work."[12]

The language of conquering enemies in this meditation might be a bit off-putting in the quest to find peace; it reeks of patriarchy and violence. So why spend time with it? Why not ignore it, confine it to a past where such language was acceptable? That would be too easy, and we'd be worse off for such a quick dismissal. After all, we've already discussed the importance of reframing texts for the work of peace. Let's do so here. This meditation offers the necessary entrance into the upside-down world that our engagement with a cannonball moment demands. We look to Christ as our mentor figure who will teach us how to bring about a new way of living. The meditation also presents a helpful opportunity for us here in our reflection on peace and spirituality. The Kingdom Meditation is reflective of Ignatius's time period, context, and language—of course! Yes, it is overly masculine in its imagery and evokes themes of war and violence. This is why it is the perfect meditation for creativity and imagination, spiritual muscles that we've already identified as essential to peace work.

The heart of this meditation is too important to dismiss. This is why I encourage you to use it to consider Christ's invitation to peace in your life. I invite you to use the following points, compiled from the work of several writers in the Ignatian tradition, as ways to engage Christ's invitation in a creative, imaginative way. Each point seeks to deconstruct and reframe the violent assumptions written into the original meditation. Sit with each one; see if any particularly moves you. What about Christ's invitation to peace work most appeals and applies to you in this moment?

- **Beyond the "king."** Father John English reminds us that "the significance of a king is quite different from that of an ordinary leader. It has a dimension to it that makes it unique. . . . The sovereign personifies and carries the whole nation."[13] Christ, then, as "king" isn't simply a leader; Christ, as king, holds together the entirety of the cosmos, all of creation. We are reminded of the first incarnation, when God created *everything*. This "call" orients us not simply toward a ruler but toward the entirety of God's vision. To respond to the Call of Christ is to respond to the cries of the earth and the cries of the poor—and to take a cosmic perspective. Drawing on the legacy of Pierre Teilhard de Chardin, whom we met in chapter 1, Louis Savary writes, "While some describe the grace for this meditation as to 'fall in love with Jesus,' Teilhard would have you also ask for the grace to fall in love with the cosmos. While Ignatius focuses on the Christ of the Gospels, Teilhard's focus is also on the Christ of the Cosmos."[14]

How does Christ as unifier, as manifestation of all creation, inspire a life of peace? Do you see all things as working together through Christ to bring about Christ's vision of peace, justice, and compassion? How does this view of Christ in all and through all encourage you to recognize all things as invitations to contemplate peace? What does Christ in all mean for our reordering of relationships?

- **More than a "call."** Father David Fleming challenges the use of the word *call*, which he says "does not capture well the quality of the initiative taken by God or by Christ. Jesus does not issue an invitation or call in which he has no personal feeling. . . . He puts his whole self into the call."[15] We should be shaken by and in awe of this fact: Christ *desires* our collaboration. Christ has asked *us* to share in the work of love and peace, the reordering of relationships so as to build a more just society. "Ignatius is insistent on our unity with Christ—our sharing the work, pain and victory of Jesus," writes English. We are given full agency to *respond in love*. "It is intended to stir up generosity and awareness of Christ's call. . . . It involves an offering of ourselves to be with Jesus in his work."[16]

Christ uniquely desires you, me, each person in the work of peace. Christ desires our full selves and our unique selves—insights, experiences, relationships, magis. How does Christ's invitation reframe our strengths and our weaknesses? How does Christ's delight in us stir up generosity?

- **Centering the parable.** Words like *kingdom*, *king*, and *conquer*—all words used in this particular meditation—were useful in the past but certainly can alienate some people today. "By confronting the historical limitations, it is possible to discover a parable that today, as yesterday, has possibilities for transformation by posing these questions," write Katherine Dyckman, Mary Garvin, and Elizabeth Liebert in *The Spiritual Exercises Reclaimed*. "Does this image free us to find God? Could it help us find God in the future?" To this end, as we reflect on the kind of worldly leader that attracts and inspires us, we imagine "a person who unleash[es] one's admiration and loyalty in a relationship that elicit[s] 'greatness.'"[17]

What language helps you better encounter God? What language hinders that relationship—and thus your own efforts to build up God's dream of peace? How are you being invited to transcend that language?

- **Radically inclusive.** Christ is not a ruler for some; he is a lover of all. The Christ project is eternally relevant. "Faith affirms that God's Reign irrupts into this world and advances in the heart of history," writes Dean Brackley. "Christ invites people of every time and place to participate."[18] The work Christ labors for is centered on justice, truth, and peace. Rather than subject people against their will, Christ invites. "Ignatius is talking about covering the planet with people exuding unconditional love. It is only love that will conquer. . . . Ignatius' kingdom meditation is really a parable about the power and attraction of real love on the human heart, more than about kings and knights."[19]

How do we each see our individual vocations as part of this universal mission of love in action? How does our inclusive love bring about a new world of peace and compassion? What unique contribution do you offer? How does Christ respond?

- **Nothing is impossible.** Isaiah 11 paints a picture of the upside-down utopia that Christ desires:

> Then the wolf shall be a guest of the lamb,
>   and the leopard shall lie down with the young goat;
> the calf and the young lion shall browse together,
>   with a little child to guide them.
> The cow and the bear shall graze, together
>   their young shall lie down;
>   the lion shall eat hay like the ox.
> The baby shall play by the viper's den,
>   and the child lay his hand on the adder's lair.
> They shall not harm or destroy on all my holy
>   mountain;
>   for the earth shall be filled with knowledge of the
>   LORD,
>   as water covers the sea. (Isa. 11:6–9)

What a wonderful world that would be! But as Father Brian McDermott, SJ, pointed out in a homily at the Carmelite monastery near my home in Towson, Maryland, such a world, to our logical thinking, is impossible. The lion *needs* to eat the calf for survival. Wolves and lambs aren't just enemies; they are part of the natural food chain. But Christ invites us to imagine something more; Christ challenges the very boundaries of what is possible—and breaks them. Do our aspirations for peace reflect this boldness?

How does Christ's call sustain us in work that often feels impossible? From integrating our own anxious selves to bridging communities torn apart by hate, peace work can seem a fool's errand. Does Christ's depiction of peace inspire you? Challenge you? Draw you into the Christ project, even in all its mystery? Why?

In the end, this meditation challenges us to allow the Spirit to expand our understanding of the cosmic Christ who beckons us into the work of love and peace, who labors *with* us to realize God's dream. As Brackley writes, "What is the cause to which Christ calls us? And who is Christ, who calls? Ignatius could count on a common understanding of the cause, that is, God's saving work and the mission of the church. We cannot presume that today. . . . people are skeptical of saviors."[20]

How do we reimagine the invitation in a way that is inclusive, inspiring, and reflective of the God who desires our full flourishing? Are we courageous enough to allow the Spirit to push at the boundaries of our imaginations?

Make a Return

Just a few years after my first trip to Bosnia and Herzegovina, I returned once more. I was again part of a group of colleagues from Catholic Relief Services, but this time I went to document the third gathering of the Advancing Interreligious Peacebuilding initiative. Colleagues from Egypt, the Philippines, Kenya, Bosnia and Herzegovina, and more came together to share insights for peace from their own context and collaborate to imagine a new way of manifesting peace in the world.

It was a poignant time. On the very ground upon which so much blood had been shed, new seeds of peace were being planted and nurtured. This was a personal journey for many of my colleagues, a continued discovery of their own vocation. At the same time, it was a communal endeavor: peace, necessarily built and maintained through the work of many hands. The way forward was covered in a thick layer of mist, but the proverbial cannonball strike that had devastated Bosnia and Herzegovina and so many of the other communities from which my colleagues came demanded ongoing action, even if only in hesitant, staggering steps. Part of that journey required a circling back to the very place the cannonball had destroyed.

This is an essential insight for peacebuilding—whether within ourselves or within our communities. Peace is not a linear path: We stumble off the road, we double back, we check the map and try again. But we keep going. We look past the status quo and brave the upside-down world, always eager to learn from a wise sage—Jesus, of course, but also the many wisdom figures in our own lives—who embodies the very best of that upside-down world. After all, it's the only place in which we might find hope for a better world. When the status quo simply won't do, we have to turn things on their head.

"Accepting vulnerability, we must risk the step into the unknown and unpredictable lands and seek constructive engagement with those people and things we least understand and most fear," John Paul Lederach reflects. "We must take up the inevitably perilous but absolutely necessary journey that makes its way back to humanity and the building of genuine community."[21]

Joseph Campbell reminds us, too, that any hero's journey requires a circling back, a return to the community from which we set out. But we return changed, with the lessons learned from the upside-down world. We look again to Christ who went out from God only to then return to God, the very same cyclical, mythic journey. We are given a reminder, then, that we don't build peace solely for ourselves: The peace we have is the peace we share with others, the peace with which we are gifted so that we may give that same gift to the ones who most need it.

A Spiritual Exercise for Peace Work

Opening Prayer

Pray for the grace to recognize more clearly Christ's unique call to peace in your life.

Prayer Text

The people who walked in darkness
    have seen a great light;
Upon those who lived in a land of gloom
    a light has shone.
You have brought them abundant joy
    and great rejoicing;
They rejoice before you as people rejoice at harvest,
    as they exult when dividing the spoils.
For the yoke that burdened them,
    the pole on their shoulder,
The rod of their taskmaster,
    you have smashed, as on the day of Midian.
For every boot that tramped in battle,
    every cloak rolled in blood,
    will be burned as fuel for fire.
For a child is born to us, a son is given to us;
    upon his shoulder dominion rests.

They name him Wonder-Counselor, God-Hero,
    Father-Forever, Prince of Peace.
His dominion is vast
    and forever peaceful,
Upon David's throne, and over his kingdom,
    which he confirms and sustains
By judgment and justice,
    both now and forever.

Isaiah 9:1–6

Reflection Exercises

- Prayerfully read the passage above. Do you see the movement from cannonball strike to Christ's call to the upside-down world to the impossible-made-possible? Find yourself in this text: When did darkness in your life give way to a glimmer of light? What was the source of that shift? What happened next?

- What about the prayer text resonates with your journey from cannonball to call? What about it unsettles you?

Conversation

- Choose a line from the passage that stands out to you. In conversation with God or with neighbor, discuss what that line means, why it jumps out and how it might inspire you in your own journey of peace.

- God promises to smash the yoke, pole, or rod that is being used to oppress us. Ask God: Are *we* unknowingly holding such an instrument in our hands over another? How might God be trying to stop *us* from inadvertently engaging in some form of oppression?

Journal

- Spend time reflecting on the names the prayer text gives to Christ. Does one in particular speak to you? Why? Are there names you would add? Which ones? What do they point to? How does the name you would bestow upon Christ uniquely reflect the call Christ has made to you?

CHAPTER 5

Incarnation

When Peace Draws Near

The Grinch steals Christmas—this we know. But the story of the Grinch doesn't begin with him prowling about *Who*-ville. Dr. Seuss is quite clear that the Grinch "lived just north of *Who*-ville," and from that vantage point, "he stood there on Christmas Eve, hating the *Whos*, staring down from his cave with a sour, Grinchy frown at the warm lighted windows below in their town."[1]

This, I believe, is important. As we begin this chapter, I want us to hold in our minds this image of staring down upon a scene. The scene in question necessarily unsettles us—or, by its very nature, is simply *unsettling*. Grinches and nongrinches alike are unsettled, and what we find unsettling can move us to action. But do we let it?

This movement to action is in many ways the story of Christmas. The advent of God's breaking into the history of creation begins with a long, loving, unsettling look. Incarnation is the response. Incarnation—God's own through Jesus but also the invitation God holds out to us to make God known in the world—is what this chapter is all about. What do we do *after* we've taken that long, loving look? How do we respond to scenes that we find unsettling? How does God respond?

We all see scenes each day that lack the peace we desire. These scenes play out in communities around the world, across news headlines, within heavily fortified meeting rooms, in our own homes, and in our own hearts. What do we do with this feeling of unease?

Incarnation Now!

The Second Week of the Spiritual Exercises is a close meditation on the life of Christ. We pray through Jesus's earthly ministry, companioning with him as he heals and serves and loves—as he shows us the upside-down world, what it means to live and love in a radically unsettling way. Ignatius, ultimately, wants us to come to know Jesus as our friend. The grace we ask for as we pray through the Second Week of meditations is "an intimate knowledge of our Lord, who has become [human] for me, that I may love him more and follow him more closely."[2]

The Second Week naturally begins with the story of the Incarnation. It's here that Ignatius calls us to pay close attention to the holy gaze of the Trinity. "The Three Divine Persons look down upon the whole expanse or circuit of all the earth, filled with human beings," Ignatius reminds us. Then, in what almost sounds a bit tongue-in-cheek, he says, "Since they see that all are going down to hell, they decree in their eternity that the Second Person should become man to save the human race."[3] Ignatius encourages us to contemplate Mary and the particular time and place in which the angel Gabriel meets her.

Then Ignatius circles back, inviting us to join with the Trinity in gazing upon the world. Ignatius wants us to see what God sees, to understand deeply what God finds unsettling. While the notion of God "looking down" is perhaps a bit outdated—after all, God had made all things, works through all things, and thus can be encountered through all things and not simply on some cloud in the sky—I still find this imagery helpful. We can imagine ourselves gazing down upon a scene, one from which we are wholly removed and yet deeply affected by the goings-on.

Ignatius is clear that there is great diversity across the planet, "in dress and in manner of acting"—and God sees and loves this. There are so many people, "some at peace, and some at war; some weeping, some laughing; some well, some sick; some coming into the world, and some dying." The Trinity looks "down upon the whole surface of the earth, and behold[s] all nations in great blindness, going down to death and descending into hell."[4]

What is causing the whole creation to descend to hell? Ignatius points specifically to the violent tendencies of humanity. "What the Divinity observes is horrific," writes my friend, Jesuit Robert McChesney, whom we've met before. "A world swearing, blaspheming, wounding, killing, going to hell and so on."[5] Violence in word and deed, and we're blind to it, to its scope and its long-term impact on God's universe. The Incarnation—through God, for all of creation—is the antidote.

It's easy to allow ourselves to be put off by the expression "going to hell," but I think we can leave the theological implication aside and simply *look* at our world. Many people are *already* living in hell, and the actions of a few seem to send more and more people to such darkness each day. We can look at the children who go to bed hungry, the communities that fear the next falling bomb, the debilitating loneliness of an elderly neighbor, the fear created by speech riddled with hate, and the systemic oppression experienced by so many people of color. All these scenes and so many more reflect something *hellish*. And they should unsettle. Certainly, such fear and division and uncertainty and distrust unsettle our *society*—shaking the very foundation of peace. But too often, we are blind, as Ignatius reminds us, to what's really going on around us, to how it's impacting people and our own shared future.

Father McChesney, in his essay "Noticing *Hibakusha*: A Trauma-Informed Reading of the Incarnation Contemplation," meditates on the example of Father Pedro Arrupe, the twenty-eighth superior general of the Society of Jesus. It was Arrupe who would reinvigorate the Jesuits in their gospel call to justice and peace. But before becoming the Society's global leader, Arrupe served on the outskirts of Hiroshima, Japan, in 1945. He lived through the nuclear bombing and in its immediate aftermath, he ministered to hundreds of victims. Such trauma forever impacted his life—how could it not? "Proximity to Ground Zero was crucial, a lesson [Arrupe] would never forget," McChesney writes.[6] Arrupe, like his fellow Basque Jesuit predecessor, Ignatius of Loyola, was indelibly marked by his proximity to violence.

What does this mean for the Incarnation, for us, and for our own reflections on finding peace? Return to that initial idea of gazing down upon a scene. That's what God is doing, no? God is taking that long, loving look at the real. But God doesn't stop there. God *needs* to get involved. God has to get into the mix, get close to all that pain and suffering. God's very nature demands an entering into the chaos, a drawing near to the violence. There is no salvation without this movement.

That's the story of the Incarnation, which reveals that God draws ever nearer to suffering, closer and closer to ground zero. Again, we have to remind ourselves that we are made in the image and likeness of this same God.

Downward Mobility

I can be a rather anxious person. And few events manifest my anxiety like the weeks and days leading up to international travel.

Such travel for me has rarely been a trip to a luxury resort. In my work at Catholic Relief Services and for the Jesuit Conference of Canada and the United States, I have had the privilege of traveling to places that are off the beaten path. I usually go to gather stories that otherwise go untold. I've visited farming communities in Vietnam, remote villages in Haiti, and schools in Sierra Leone miles away from any paved roads. I've slept on gym floors in Portugal, on library floors in Spain, and—despite my protests—on the only bed in a two-room home of a family of four in the Philippines. I've taken bucket showers and malaria medication. These trips are often incredible but rarely what one would call *comfortable.*

Having worked in nonprofit communications for some time, I can safely say that there are people who are made for this kind of travel, this kind of exploration. I can also safely say I am not one of those people. That's where the anxiety kicks in.

Will I get lost? Make my connections? Find my host? I fret over what I should pack, how much I should pack, and how my packing will be perceived by others. I check the weather and the possibility for disease, triple-check my documents, print out my boarding passes and every email I've received about my itinerary. I worry over whether or not I'm qualified to go on the trip, if it's worth leaving my family, if it's worth the financial investment of my sponsoring organization, and on and on.

At some point before departure, I even wonder, "Why do I do this to myself?" If I really wanted to, I could avoid these trips. Send someone else. Take a different job. Conduct interviews remotely. Travel to more comfortable places. There are usually ways around these expeditions.

But time and time again, I go. Even now, as I write these words, I'm planning a trip that I know will make me anxious as the date draws nearer. No one is telling me to go; I'm seeking out these opportunities. Something drives me to do so. But what? Why do I do this to myself?

It's an important question, particularly as the environmental cost of flying across the world adds up. Not to mention the general absurdity of another white American guy showing up in communities in one country after another to take photos and write stories. Why do I do this?

It's the same question I asked myself during those many months of postgraduate service in Bolivia. The answer then and now is this: Because I was responding to *something*. *Something* invites me to keep doing this, to keep working in this field, to keep seeking out these trips. I know I add very little tangible value: I'm not a doctor or an engineer or an aid worker. While the stories I produce may be good, they're not vital.

The answer to the question isn't about the *outcome*—at least, not completely. It's about the *experience*. It's about something within me that calls out to something within the world. It's me looking at that same world, gazing intently upon creation in all its many forms, and desiring to draw near. To leave the comfortable. To enter the uncomfortable. And, most importantly, to share in that moment with others.

Made in the image and likeness of a God who feels compelled to enter into the uncomfortable, to be in that space, to form relationships and share in joy and sorrow and success and failure—I think that's what I'm responding to.

Have you felt the desire to descend to the real stuff of life, with all its suffering and discomfort? Perhaps it doesn't manifest itself in international travel, but there are countless other ways in which we set aside our comfort to enter into discomfort, to stand alongside others existing in that discomfort. That desire, I believe, can be so strong that it beats out our natural aversion to discomfort, the parts of us that say, "No! Wait! Not that!"—my anxiety, for example.

We respond to the call to enter into that which is uncomfortable in so many ways—or, at least, we are given the chance to. We pause to help someone struggling with the ticket machine instead of rushing to catch our train—and risk being late. We volunteer at our kid's school party and take a few hours off work—and risk missing an important email. We make casseroles for the soup kitchen instead of solely cooking meals for ourselves—and risk having to eat something a bit simpler for dinner. We call our elected officials to advocate for more just policies instead of simply observing news via headlines—and risk an awkward conversation.

There are so many opportunities, big or small, consequential or just personally fulfilling, in which we are called to risk discomfort. To give up a little of ourselves, of our time and energy and resources. In so doing, we go to others.

This is, in some small way, our participation in the Incarnation. The essence of the Incarnation is captured in the Greek word *kenōsis*, best articulated in Paul's letter to the Philippians where he reminds us that Christ "emptied" himself; Christ "humbled" himself (2:7, 8). The Second Person of the Trinity willingly gives up the comfort of being God to step into the discomfort of being human. "If there is any encouragement in Christ," Paul writes, "Do nothing out of selfishness or out of vainglory; rather, humbly regard others as more important than yourselves, each looking out not for his own interests, but [also] everyone for those of others" (2:1, 3–4). We give up something of ourselves, making space in ourselves for the lives of others. We are made in the image and likeness of a God who does exactly this.

Jesuit priest Dean Brackley, whom we were introduced to in the last chapter, writes about this in his essential work, *The Call to Discernment in Troubled Times*. He says this trajectory of God is the way of Christ, or, by another name, downward mobility. It is a path marked by poverty, contempt, and humility—quite unattractive features, if we're being honest. "In traditional societies with little social mobility, the typical security strategy was to keep your head down and snuggle up to a powerful protector," he writes. "In modern societies, the most common strategy is upward social mobility."[7] We climb and climb this ladder in the hopes that we'll get richer, more popular, want for nothing, and—ultimately—be safe. But this is a lie. "We are awakening to the disquieting fact that it is impossible for everyone, or even the majority, to enjoy the affluent lifestyle of the world's middle classes."[8] For there to be winners in this particular game, there have to be losers. If I get that promotion, you don't. If I buy that house, you can't have it. If I use up that resource, it won't be available to future generations.

So we fight. We fight to win the bidding war, to prove ourselves the best employee, and to gain control over coveted resources. We fight to demonstrate that we are the most impressive, best dressed, happiest person on the planet. We fight ourselves, trying to convince ourselves that we *can* be happy if we get that next thing: a bit of praise, a new job, a bigger fence. We win the fight only when we find ourselves in complete *control*, because when we're in control, we feel comfortable. This fighting, as we so easily see, can become quite literal and quite deadly.

"To seek security through control of our surroundings dehumanizes us and destroys our environment," Brackley says. How many human lives are sacrificed in the pursuit of so-called security? Can such security, such complete control, actually ever be achieved—or is it a lie we tell ourselves as we rabidly engage in arms races of all kinds? "The alternative strategy is faith, by which we abandon ourselves to God's care. Faith allows us to let things go and share what we have."[9] Instead of one of us being the best, we both collaborate toward a common goal.

Thus we begin to see the logic of the downward mobility of Christ, of the Incarnation itself. If we constantly climb upward, higher and higher into the status quo of our world, we will find ourselves both constantly looking over our shoulder and glancing up ahead. Is someone about to catch up? To overtake us?

Will they be better, smarter, more attractive than us? How much further ahead can we get, *must* we get in order to be happy and safe and secure? We construct the illusion of happiness with an abundance of comfort, and we fortify our castle. No one can touch us. Yet we clearly have no real peace.

This mentality doesn't only breed cold wars on the geopolitical stage. It also creates a coldness within us. The more we have, the more we need to protect. The more we want, the more we get, the more we build up our own little empire. Then we fear to lose what we have, so we need to protect what we have—and get more to prove our ongoing worth. To what end will we go to continue this spiral?

This is the world the Trinity gazes upon. It's no wonder it's hellish. Comfort isn't inherently a bad thing—God loves us, and so we are lovable and deserving of all the good things God desires to give. We must love ourselves. Jesus himself reminds us that we can love our neighbors *only if* we properly love ourselves (see Matt. 22:39). We aren't called to discomfort for discomfort's sake. We're called to enter into our shared humanity, to accompany one another. Discomfort just so happens to often be the road sign that gets us where we're going. But when we get so caught up in our own *stuff*, in creating for ourselves and our inner circle a life of absolute comfort, then we go awry. We stay put and we stay miserable, because we are made in the image and likeness of a God who does not *reject* comfort but who is eager and willing to enter into *discomfort* and so draw nearer to the beating heart of creation.

Incarnation as Beauty

I want to stress this point: God does not desire our perpetual discomfort. I am not advocating that we flagellate ourselves, sleep on a bare box spring, or eat only porridge (unless you love porridge, I guess). We may be tempted to run ourselves ragged in the service of others, forever uncomfortable, forever forgetting that all-important commandment to love ourselves, and consequently forever wrestling with resentment, bitterness, and exhaustion.

But I do hope we can see how obsessing over attaining and maintaining comfort—more money, more glamour, more stuff—can lead us down a path that leads to fear and violence, a path of perpetual competition and one-upping. An arms race of sorts.

Christ points us in a different direction by way of the Incarnation. The Incarnation itself can be seen as a call to *disarmament*. We give up not just *stuff* but *control*—and, importantly, control over the outcome, over a shot at *winning*. Made in the image and likeness of our God of kenosis, we empty ourselves; we humble ourselves. We make ourselves vulnerable like a baby in a cold, hard manger—and in that vulnerability, we realize we need others. We depend on others. Stripped of control and in all our vulnerability, we realize what we need is community.

We accept that we can't completely control our future—our future wealth, our future beauty, our future fame—and instead stay present in the *now*. We trust that, in taking care of ourselves and our neighbors, we will have what we need when the moment arises. There's no need to fight for what we think we deserve; we simply accept and share what we have.

So we turn to another incarnation—God's *first* incarnation. "God first made creation sacred about fourteen billion years ago at the Big Bang in the first moment of the universe's life," writes Louis M. Savary, an expert on the scientist and mystic Pierre Teilhard de Chardin. "About two thousand years ago, God made creation doubly sacred by a second Big Bang, which was the appearance of Jesus Christ. . . . The two are closely related because the two are different forms of incarnation, two different visible expressions of God's creativity and love."[10]

The act of creation is an incarnation of Godself. All creation is saturated in God's grace, so when we look at creation—people, plants, animals, landscapes—we see something of God. Again, we return to that all-important act of *looking*. Just as God looks at nothingness and births creation, as God looks at us and, through us, births Christ anew, so too we *look* at creation and wonder how we might manifest Christ. "A primary reason for the Incarnation is that God wanted to reveal to us that everything God created in the universe—literally every thing and every process—is sacred and holy and lives in Christ," Savary writes.[11] "For Teilhard, both the cosmos and the Christ were expressions of God's Word."[12]

We've already met Teilhard in these pages. Why is he relevant here? "[He] became well known as a writer on science and religion and on the place of Christianity in the modern world, reinterpreted in the light of evolution," writes Ursula King in her introduction to a short collection of writings by Teilhard himself.[13] At the heart of his spirituality "is a deep, intimate, and extraordinarily vibrant love of Christ—the human Jesus and the Christ of the cosmos, the ever greater, ever present Christ, the touch of whose hands we encounter deeply within all things."[14]

I want to propose that the incarnation reveals two things about God and our spirituality of peace. We've already spent much time reflecting on the Incarnation we celebrate at Christmas: the birth of Jesus, the movement of God from comfort into discomfort. But the first incarnation, the creation of the universe, reveals something equally important: beauty, wonder, and awe. While a trajectory of discomfort, or the downward mobility of Christ, helps us to shed those things that evoke fear and violence, this trajectory toward beauty and wonder helps us to celebrate and bask in the simple, ordinary moments of life's delight.

Put a different way, walking the way of discomfort brings us into community; walking the way of beauty gives us something wonderful to share together. Remembering that we are made for beauty tempers any tendency toward self-flagellation: We are worthy; we are wonderful. But so is everyone else! How might we share this beauty?

In all of this, we encounter the incarnate Christ. "Christ is not something added to the world as an extra, he is not an embellishment, a king as we now crown kings, the owner of a great estate," Teilhard insists. "He is the Alpha and the Omega, the principle and the end, the foundation stone and the keystone."[15] We often think of Jesus as coming at Christmas some two thousand years ago. But of course, Christ has always been; Christ is the Second Person of the Trinity. That's why Teilhard speaks of a "Christified universe" in which "God can in the future be experienced and apprehended by the whole ambient totality of what we call evolution—*in Christo Jesu.*"[16]

Why would we stay in our own little bubbles of comfort and security when *everything* out there is revealing God's dream for creation? The call to discomfort is an invitation into the ever-unfolding life of Christ in community and in communion with all of creation. Has God placed that discomfort in our own hearts as a propulsion to get us out of our status quo lives and into the great beating heart of the cosmos? What might we learn if we respond to that discomfort? What invitation might we be able to answer?

Perhaps this is why I push against my own anxious tendencies to go to faraway places and bear witness to people far different from me: God is calling me into something more. And God is calling *you*. The temptation to stay put, to cling to the way things are, to fight and defend some dying status quo is not the way to peace. It is the way to unnecessary violence and ultimately decay.

The Grinch Who Shared Christmas

Let's return to the Grinch.

If we really are made in the image and likeness of a God who gets involved, who is moved by what is seen, entering deeply into the moment so as to remind us again and again of our own beauty, then we are called to do the same—even at our grinchiest. When we have no peace within ourselves, I wonder if that's not exactly the moment to remember and respond to the invitation of the Incarnation. Lean in and find the beauty. Then, point it out to someone else. Bask in that shared beauty together.

I often come back to C. S. Lewis's definition of friendship from his book *The Four Loves*. Friendship depends on a common interest, on seeing something *together*. It rests on the expression, as Lewis notes, of "What? You too? I thought I was the only one." There is a necessary seeing and sharing, a willingness to enter into the life of another by giving something of your own. "We can imagine that among those early hunters and warriors, single individuals saw what others did not; saw that the deer was beautiful as well as edible, that hunting was fun as well as necessary, dreamed that his gods might be not only powerful but holy. . . . It is when two such persons discover one another, when, whether with immense difficulties and semi-articulate fumblings or with what would seem to us amazing and elliptical speed, they share their vision—it is then that Friendship is born. And instantly they stand together in an immense solitude."[17]

As we end this chapter, I encourage you to reflect on the people in your life whom you might be invited to look at more deeply. We are made in the image and likeness of a God who gazed upon all creation and desired to enter into the story. Who are the friends, family, colleagues, strangers in your life into whose story you can enter more intimately? Are you being invited to manifest Christ in a unique way for another person? I think the answer is necessarily yes. That's the unfolding story of the Incarnation! But none of us can do so if we are focused solely on ourselves, on holding tightly to control over our things, our reputation, our ego. We have to surrender something of ourselves—we have to risk discomfort—to encounter the story of another. Then, we might truly see that other person in all their wonder and need.

A Spiritual Exercise for Peace Work

Opening Prayer

Pray for the grace to discover in God's invitation how your unique call to discomfort and beauty might birth peace.

Prayer Text

Do nothing out of selfishness or out of vainglory; rather, humbly regard others as more important than yourselves, each looking out not for his own interests, but [also] everyone for those of others.

Have among yourselves the same attitude that is also yours in Christ Jesus,

> Who, though he was in the form of God,
> > did not regard equality with God something to be grasped.
> Rather, he emptied himself,
> taking the form of a slave,
> coming in human likeness;
> and found human in appearance,
> he humbled himself,
> > becoming obedient to death,

even death on a cross.
Because of this, God greatly exalted him.
Philippians 2:3–9

Reflection Exercises

- This passage from Scripture clearly and visually reflects Christ's downward mobility. How do words like "emptied" and "humbled" strike you in your own spiritual journey? What role do you believe they have in our shared work for peace?

- The instances of incarnation we've reflected on in this chapter are simply God revealing Godself in a physical way within our world. Have you ever considered the role *you* might be called to play in God's desire to manifest Godself in the world? How might you—both body and soul—manifest God's desire for peace?

Conversation

- In conversation with God or with neighbor, talk about your own sources of discomfort. How might they instead be seen as holy invitations? What might God be trying to reveal?

- Do you find yourself tempted to go too far in discomfort—burning yourself out or running yourself ragged? Do you believe God desires this for you? How can you balance in your life both discomfort and God's delight in you?

Journal

- Spend time meditating on sources of beauty present in your day. How is God's Spirit of peace at work in these moments? How might you share them with others? Name the moments and the people with whom you'd like to share them.

CHAPTER 6

Two Standards, Two Directions

Once upon a time there was a wise and benevolent ruler who presided over a flourishing land and was beloved by all who lived there. For many years, the people lived in peace: Bellies were full, young minds were trained, and neighboring communities looked on in wonder and awe. As a result, the citizens of that land were happy and never questioned their leader or his decisions.

The leader loved the people. He considered it his sacred duty to provide for and protect them. Having come from a war-torn land where he lost his own family to violence, he had pledged long ago never again to let such evil befall those he loved. He committed to do whatever he had to do to ensure peace reigned supreme.

This meant training in body and mind to meet the moment whenever it arose. He studied the arts of magic and politics alike, and he soon became regarded as a powerful sorcerer. It was his hard-earned magical prowess that gave this leader the ability to protect his people. That same magic allowed him to provide for all, to grant wishes and inspire devotion.

After long years, he had built a utopia. He had accomplished what he'd always dreamed. He had made good on the promise he'd made to himself, and he had the love of many to affirm him in his decisions.

One day he was met with a challenge in the form of an inquisitive young woman. Were all of his decisions truly good? she wondered. Was the land in fact one of peace? Or was there a hidden threat of violence that held the whole facade together? Was the beloved leader actually enforcing his own vision through magic and power without truly listening to the people? Was he suppressing the true wishes of those he ruled to maintain a fragile peace?

These questions were too much. The leader felt threatened, so he doubled down on his magic, on his power. He sought more of it, consulted forbidden texts. Suddenly, he became the villain.

This parable (if you take out the magical elements) can map onto so many moments, from our personal stories to our history textbooks to headlines across the internet: A once beloved and benevolent leader suddenly feels threatened and, as a result, becomes defensive, turning inward and hoarding power. We see it in world leaders; we see it in power-hungry bosses; we see it in jealous romantic partners; we may see it in ourselves.

What might surprise us, though, is how unexpected that turn to villainy can feel. How does benevolence become spite? How do good and worthy intentions result in sorrow and destruction and death? Outwardly, everything appeared right and just, but inwardly, something went terribly awry. To the unobservant, this is jarring. Without warning, it seems, a land of tranquility and justice is suddenly cast into conflict and chaos. What happened?

Answering these questions will be the focus of this chapter. The fruits of good and evil are often most clearly seen through the peace or violence that follows. Too often in our lives and in our world, violence seems to explode out of nowhere. But if we're paying attention, if we're reading the signs, we might be able to detect when evil masquerades as good and when violence pretends to be peace. Central to the experience of Ignatian spirituality and the Spiritual Exercises is a meditation called the Two Standards in which Ignatius gives us tools to parse good from bad long before the explosion of conflict. As is true for all these Ignatian mediations, this one is accessible and relevant for each of us, no matter our faith tradition or our familiarity with the Exercises.

We'll come back to that parable, too, because it's illustrative. If you've seen the 2023 animated Disney film *Wish*, the plot points probably sound familiar. King Magnifico is a prime example of a leader who appears wholly benevolent until—seemingly with little warning—he isn't. We'll talk more about him and how we can avoid his fate.

Just Give Me Two Signs

The Two Standards Meditation falls squarely in the Second Week of the Spiritual Exercises. It uses language and imagery that we might find a bit outdated, even uncomfortable. After all, what exactly *is* a "standard," and why would I need two of them? Imagine yourself gazing at a battle scene, two warring camps opposite each other beneath billowing banners—those banners are the standards. In this battle, the stakes are quite high. And we can't remain observers; we must pick a side.

Ignatius sets the scene like this: "Christ calls and wants all beneath his standard, and Lucifer, on the other hand, wants all under his. This is the mental representation of the place. It will be here to see a great plain, comprising the whole region about Jerusalem, where the sovereign Commander-in-Chief of all the good is Christ our Lord; and another plain about the region of Babylon, where the chief of the enemy is Lucifer."[1]

Ignatius, as usual, wants us to imagine ourselves there alongside the combatants. To feel what it's like. To watch the shuffling feet of the soldiers. To smell the sweat and fear. We then listen to the address made by the enemy to those in his camp: "He goads them on to lay snares for [all] and bind them with chains. First, they are to tempt them to covet riches that they may the more easily attain the empty honors of this world, and then come to overweening pride."[2] The standard of the enemy, then, is represented by riches, honors, and pride. More specifically, we find ourselves *beneath* that standard when we are inordinately *attached* to riches, honors, and pride. These are the chains with which the enemy tries to bind us. We seek more money not so we can give back to others but so we can amass more goods for ourselves; we seek out honors not so we can use our position to benefit the vulnerable but so we can draw more attention to our own accomplishments.

As the great Jesuit spiritual director Father Joe Tetlow reminds us, the progression under the enemy's standard is this: "Look at all this stuff I have" to "Look at me with all this stuff" to "Look at *me*."[3] Swollen pride is the final step. Pride, of course, isn't necessarily evil—neither are money or praise. But as Father Dean Brackley reminds us, in this case "*pride* means believing not just that we are important (we are, after all), but that we are more important than others."[4] And when we view ourselves as the only thing that matters, or even the most important thing, how slippery is the slope to hatred, violence, and suffering—the lengths to which we might go to preserve our self-importance.

We eliminate not only other people from the equation but also God. We become so obsessed with ourselves that our ability to make good choices in and for the world diminishes. We are reduced to making choices that benefit only us. We become awash in fear over what we might lose: our stuff, our wealth, the attention of others, the praise we've grown so accustomed to. We find ourselves huddled on a lonely island.

But what about Christ's standard? We listen to Jesus's words, an address made to "his servants and friends whom he sends on this enterprise, recommending to them to seek to help all, first by attracting them to the highest spiritual poverty . . . to a desire for insults and contempt, for from these springs humility."[5] The standard of Christ is all about poverty, rejection, and humility—not the most compelling reason to join a community, to be sure! We see here the Ignatian call to cultivate a disposition of indifference, to hold all things lightly so as to avoid allowing any one thing to hold *us* too tightly. We make constant room for others, recognizing in one another our shared belovedness, our common call to walk with Christ. It's important here to highlight that Christ speaks to us as friends. We journey *together.* We build up a shared vision, one in which solidarity and community are celebrated. No one beneath the standard of Christ ends up on a lonely island.

The Two Standards Meditation is not simply a onetime decision-making tool. It's a lens through which we see the world, a framework against which we make constant decisions: Am I taking this new job simply to make more money, or can I do genuine good in this role? Am I upset because a real injustice has been committed at work, or is my pride wounded because a colleague correctly called me to task? If I continue to participate in this conversation, will I be able to shed light on truth, or will I become consumed by gossip that makes me feel important? And so on.

"Ascertaining what is life-giving or death-dealing to self and others remains a continual challenge," write Katherine Dyckman, Mary Garvin, and Elizabeth Liebert in *The Spiritual Exercises Reclaimed: Uncovering Liberating Possibilities for Women.* "The underlying touchstone, of course, is always the life, death, and resurrection of Jesus and the openness to his

Spirit. But discernment in the Two Standards acts like a tuning fork for discerning the realities of life, indicating resonance or dissonance with the God who dwells within."[6]

Each decision we make gets measured against the Two Standards in an ongoing effort to ferret out the enemy's nefarious schemes. "The enemy has sown weeds throughout the wheat field of the world, weeds that look like wheat," Brackley advises. "Every person, action, and institution, every real-world project is morally ambiguous and prone to corruption."[7] If we are not intentional and discerning, we may find ourselves collaborating in that work of corruption. We've already discussed how bloated, swollen pride makes us susceptible to seeing others as less-than. The Two Standards Meditation helps us continually course correct.

War and Peace

At this point, you may be saying—much as you did with the Kingdom Meditation—"Eric, this is another war-heavy meditation for a book on peace." To that I'd say, You're not wrong. You may recall that at the outset of this book I reflected on the many times folks had told me that meditating on peace through the lens of Ignatian spirituality was a fool's errand. This meditation—one in which we place ourselves in the scene of battle—is perhaps the most glaring reason.

But there's something going on here that demands our attention. The enemy goads his "troops" on and into the world to sow havoc. The enemy cares little for these supposed foot soldiers; the enemy desires only that they create discord, loneliness, and pain. This quest for inordinate riches, constant honor, and swollen pride necessarily pushes people deeper and deeper into the enemy's camp. It ensnares them. How? The enemy convinces us that our value is based solely on what we have—and we can never have enough. The enemy tells us we must be the best, and we must constantly compare ourselves to others, to what others have and do. This causes us to constantly look over our shoulder for threats from those who might be catching up. We lust after those who have more, who have done more, who appear better than us or are seemingly more valuable to society. This twisted logic justifies drastic action on our part: How far will we go to feel like we're the best, like we're successful, like we're faring better than those around us? We like how pride makes us feel, and we need to continually feel proud at all costs.

"Most of us feel proud of our achievements at first," writes psychologist Ronald Siegel in his book *The Extraordinary Gift of Being Ordinary: Finding Happiness Right Where You Are.* "The problem is, we humans (like all creatures) *habituate to everything.* We become accustomed to having what we have, and our feelings about ourselves then go up or down from our new normal."[8] Siegel goes on to say that our response is to continue to feed the inner beast: To sustain the feeling of pride, power, popularity, what have you, we need to keep seeking out the next great achievement.

"It's not just that we become accustomed to our new level of success; we develop new standards," he writes. "Sadly, as long as we're looking for achievements to make us feel good about ourselves, we're doomed to always need more and more just to feel good enough."[9] This creates a sense of desperation that none of us wants but all of us can likely relate to. Desperate people make bad choices.

Compare that to the standard of Christ, the standard of belovedness, the standard of the one who calls us as we are and invites us into intimate collaboration. In fact, if we look at the standard of Christ, I wonder if there is really any war-making going on at all. The enemy sends foot soldiers out with little thought to their well-being, but Christ calls us "friend." We are encouraged "to seek to help all."[10] We follow a path of poverty, rejection, and humility—a path that makes us more open and available to others. And the more we see of another, the more we see of ourselves in their stories and the less room we have for hate and violence. Christ's standard, I think, is meant to disarm those who would do evil. It is a standard of nonviolence. (We'll talk more about that later.)

A colleague once pushed back on the idea that a soldier like Ignatius would know little or care little for peace. She said that, on the contrary, those who have suffered most from war and conflict, who have lived enmeshed in its ruin, who have been on its frontlines, know the most about the value of peace and the lies of war. Perhaps Ignatius is a better teacher on the matter than we realize. I wonder if he hasn't embedded the key to peace in one of his most violent mediations.

We live in a world marred by violence. It only makes sense that Ignatius, realist that he is, would draw his spiritual principles from that same world while simultaneously marrying them to the life of Christ. If we look to Christ, we know that violence is inherent in the Christian story. I'm not talking about the violence done by Christians or to Christians over the ages; I'm talking about the cross, Jesus hanging there on a piece of wood, the bearer of so much violence, pain, and suffering. The crucifixion reminds us of institutionalized violence as much as it reminds us that our individual decisions can do violence to others. We see an empire that makes a show of a man's pain, and we see a crowd too frightened to speak out against it. Jesus's message was too radical. It was too much for those in power—those who were clinging to their wealth, honor, and pride—to accept that all were equally loved by God.

If everyone belongs, if everyone is equal, then all that power, all that wealth and honor and pride, does nothing to set one group over another. God desires that we see one another as siblings in God's own family; we all have the same inheritance. What we have, we are meant to share—not hoard. And if we share all that we have, do we then begin to dismantle those symbols of power? If I have as much as you, if I have access to all that you do, and if that's how God wants the world to work, then suddenly we have less to fear from one another and plenty to gain. However, this necessarily reorders societal relationships and destroys any notion of being better than another.

This was the good news Christ came to share. It earned him a place on the cross.

Still, we glimpse Christ's standard, breadcrumbs to a new way of understanding the world and our shared place therein. "Put your sword back into its sheath," Jesus tells the disciple who attempts to defend him against his betrayers. "For all who take the sword will perish by the sword" (Matt. 26:52). The way of peace, the way of Christ, reminds us that even those who betray us remain the beloved of God. Is that not what Ignatius reminds us of in the Two Standards Meditation? We are challenged to go out to help *everyone*, even while the enemy wages war. To do so, we must rid our own hearts of violence.

Make a Wish

If in Christ's example we see the breadcrumbs that lead to a spirituality of peace, then what can we deduce about the opposite path? We hear Christ whisper, "Put away that sword." But what does the enemy whisper? How do we distinguish one from the other?

"It would be simpler if 'good guys' in white hats faced off against 'bad guys' in black hats," Father Brackley remarks. "But matters are not so simple. . . . In this meditation our goal is to learn the deceits of the enemy and learn effective countermeasures to use against them."[11]

Let's return to the 2023 Disney film *Wish*. As if to underline Father Brackley's point, King Magnifico is garbed in white—he sure *looks* like a good guy. He's the one who has built the utopia, Rosas, and the one who provides so generously for the people who live there. He even uses his hard-won magical prowess to grant one citizen's wish every month. He's a good king; he's a good *guy*.

Then the young woman, Asha, confronts him over his wish-granting, and he's suddenly on his back foot. He doesn't want to entertain the idea of granting multiple wishes a month, but he also doesn't want to empower the citizenry to fulfill their *own* wishes and so remove him from the equation. He wants the power to decide which wish is worthy. He wants things to stay exactly as they are. He wants nosy little girls to stop asking questions.

We've all been there: We know what it's like to have our decisions challenged, to be forced to stop and rethink what we've done and where we're headed. It's unpleasant. It's uncomfortable. It's a direct challenge to our pride, our ego, our sense of honor, perhaps even our livelihood. But, as we've already discussed and as we likely already know from our own experiences, asking questions that challenge our status quo is good and necessary. There is no other way to progress, to learn, to grow. A stagnant status quo is deadly, in our personal and communal lives. The real question is, How do we respond to such a challenge?

For King Magnifico, and for far too many leaders the world over, the response is defensive resistance, grasping for more power, honors, and riches. Ultimately, that's what turns Magnifico from a beloved leader to a feared villain. In just a handful of scenes, he goes from wise to ruthless, consulting books on dark magic, assembling loyal allies, and hatching sinister plots. The fact that Asha finds herself in possession of magical powers doesn't help the king's state of mind.

There's more here to unpack, because as in any good story, the villain didn't start out that way. Magnifico began with good intentions, born from his own lived experience of poverty, pain, and loss. He seeks out a skill set that he wants to use to help people; we might put him under the standard of Christ right then and there! But it's clear as the story unfolds that Magnifico has an inordinate attachment to his power. He doesn't want to share the magical limelight. He doesn't want another to have the ability that he does. Rather than trust people, he tries to control them. He clings to his own way of proceeding. He doesn't dialogue with Asha or try to collaborate on their shared magical abilities. He doesn't try to understand the nuances of people's wishes. He simply holds tight to power.

As a result, Magnifico begins to hurt the citizens he once swore to protect. A desperate man makes desperate choices. Is this not what the slow, steady whispering of the evil spirit does? Is this not how we suddenly find ourselves huddled beneath the standard of the enemy? It's rarely a sudden turn to evil. Instead, it's the slow, drip-drip-drip of dark voices in our ear.

Jesuit Father Christopher Collins describes how this happens in his book *Habits of Freedom: 5 Ignatian Tools for Clearing Your Mind and Resting Daily in the Lord*. Father Collins brings us back to the temptations Jesus faces in the desert. "The Father just told Jesus that he is his beloved Son. Period." Collins writes. "But the enemy tries to distract from that by introducing a variable, a conditional question that seeks to throw things up for grabs."[12] As Collins observes, the enemy tries to tempt Jesus by using the word *if*. The enemy tries to call into question our very selves, our very identity before God. *If you are the beloved, then* . . .

"But Jesus does not fall for these manipulations. He doesn't take the bait," Collins continues. "He knows who he is and he doesn't need to prove it, and he doesn't need the Father to prove it either."[13]

Magnifico fell victim to those *ifs*: If you're all-powerful, you can't tolerate another sorcerer. If you're all-powerful, you can't allow for any nuance. If you're all-powerful, then show it—and don't let up. In life, as in *Wish*, the enemy tries to force us into either/or dichotomies. There must be a winner and a loser, and *if* you're the winner, you must prove it.

How much conflict is caused by such unnecessary posturing? How much suffering results from the lie that there must be a winner and a loser? How much does our world weep from the pain caused by false, unnecessary either/or dichotomies?

"I have called you friends," Christ says to us, "because I have told you everything I have heard from my Father" (John 15:15). Therein we see the standard of Christ: friendship, transparency, and room for all at the table.

A Spiritual Exercise for Peace Work

Opening Prayer

Pray for the grace to see clearly in your life the interplay of riches/honors/pride and poverty/rejection/humility.

Prayer Text

Then Jesus was led by the Spirit into the desert to be tempted by the devil. He fasted for forty days and forty nights, and afterwards he was hungry. The tempter approached and said to him, "If you are the Son of God, command that these stones become loaves of bread." He said in reply, "It is written:

> 'One does not live by bread alone,
> but by every word that comes forth from the mouth
> of God.'"

Then the devil took him to the holy city, and made him stand on the parapet of the temple, and said to him, "If you are the Son of God, throw yourself down. For it is written:

'He will command his angels concerning you'
   and 'with their hands they will support you,
   lest you dash your foot against a stone.'"

Jesus answered him, "Again it is written, 'You shall not put the Lord, your God, to the test.'" Then the devil took him up to a very high mountain, and showed him all the kingdoms of the world in their magnificence, and he said to him, "All these I shall give to you, if you will prostrate yourself and worship me." At this, Jesus said to him, "Get away, Satan! It is written:

'The Lord, your God, shall you worship
   and him alone shall you serve.'"

Then the devil left him and, behold, angels came and ministered to him.

Matthew 4:1–11

Reflection Exercises

- What happens if you take the part of Jesus in the Scripture passage? How does the evil spirit tempt you? Are the temptations the same or different? How do you respond?
- Do you see buried in these temptations a hint of violence? Does the evil spirit show you so-called threats to your power and comfort? If so, to what lengths might you go to protect what you have?

Conversation

- In conversation with God or with neighbor, discuss what it might mean in your life to pursue poverty, rejection, and humility. What emotions stir in you at the mention of those words? Might God be trying to reveal something to you about yourself?

- Are there elements of your life now that require course corrections? How can the Two Standards Meditation guide you in this moment?

Journal

- Using a Disney movie to illustrate a spiritual point may seem silly, but I believe that within the stories of our time lie profound spiritual truths. What movie, novel, comic, or TV show have you most recently enjoyed? Spend time writing about how the interplay of riches/honors/pride and poverty/rejection/humility reveals something important about the motivations of key characters.

CHAPTER 7

Structures Built on Sand and Violence

There is a lot to celebrate in Greta Gerwig's 2023 film *Barbie*: sharp writing, exceptional acting, a well-executed plot that succeeds in transforming a movie about a plastic toy into an international conversation about the evils of patriarchy. Plus, it's really funny. I watched it for the first time in my living room with my wife and two young daughters. Were they too young? Perhaps. But to the credit of the filmmaker and to the discredit of our society, I was happy to have my girls exposed to a story about strong women standing up to the house of cards that is the logic of the patriarchal system and the demands it places on women.

One scene in particular struck me. It's the moment when Margot Robbie as Barbie and Ryan Gosling as Ken arrive in the real world. They're all decked out in their colorful rollerblading outfits, just gliding along, happily unaware of the chaotic system they've just entered.

Everyone—men and women alike—are looking them up and down with a twisted blend of lust and envy.

"I feel kind of ill at ease," Barbie says. "I'm conscious, but it's myself that I'm conscious of."

"I'm not getting any of that," Ken replies. "I feel what can only be described as admired but not ogled. And there's no undertone of violence."

"Mine very much has an undertone of violence."[1]

That's the line that made me sit up in my chair. An *undertone* of violence. The fact that Barbie can clearly detect it while Ken is not only oblivious but blissfully unaffected by it is the key. The line points to the ills of patriarchy of course, a system in which men hold all the power and influence and women are cast aside as objects. But that line—that insight—also clearly points to the ways systemic and structural injustice cause systemic and structural *violence*. Patriarchy, racism, colonialism, and climate change—these are all structural injustices that do real violence to real people.

The questions that follow are these: Who are the victims? Who are the victimizers? Who are the winners? Who are the losers? Do the winners even recognize the violence being done? In Ken's case, the answer is clearly no—and that's the point. Barbie quickly discovers that the real world is one in which women are made to live in fear of violence, implied or actual, so that men can live in comfort, maintaining a status quo that benefits *some* at the expense of *all*.

This, of course, is not the world of peace we desire. The work of this chapter will be to explore spiritual tools that can help expose structural violence for what it is and trace the violence back to the roots that are entwined in our own hearts. We all have a part in upholding systems of injustice. We all also have a part in tearing such systems down.

Defining Terms

We often think that if we are not experiencing violence, then we must be experiencing peace. We can look inward to apply this notion: I am not anxious, I must be at peace; I am not under any pressure, I must be at peace; I am not beating myself up, I must be at peace. We can look at our communities and our world in a similar way: Is there gun violence? Drug abuse? Domestic abuse? War? These are all obvious displays of violence, and when we don't see them—or at least, when we don't see them in our own lives—we presume that we are living in a moment of peace.

This is partially right. As Johan Galtung and Graeme Mac-Queen note in their book *Globalizing God: Religion, Spirituality and Peace*, there are two concepts of peace: negative peace and positive peace. Negative peace is "the absence of violence." In war, the authors say, a ceasefire exemplifies negative peace. Hostilities have been stopped. The risk of being gunned down or bombed out is, theoretically, negated. There are "no more negative relations, but *indifferent* relations."[2] In such a state, relations stand on the brink, because while there is no violence *now*, there is also very little to prevent it from reoccurring.

Positive peace, by contrast, is "the presence of harmony, intended or not." It is a building up of relationships, of civil society, of self-confidence and self-love. "Peace, like conflict, is a *relation* between one or more parties," Galtung and MacQueen write. Negative peace and positive peace, then, "are as different as negative health—the absence of illness—and positive health, a state of mental, physical and social well-being with the capacity to handle much illness."[3] In the latter case, there is not only a movement toward flourishing but an increasing sense of resilience that might bolster a person or community in moments of backsliding. In the former case, any backsliding brings about immediate violence. Relationships collapse. Think of how quickly a ceasefire returns to open war.

Whether we're talking about peace within ourselves or within our communities, the more we strengthen relationships—our relationships with self, with and among others, with God and creation—the more we build the infrastructure of peace. If we stop at negative peace, we continue to live on the knife's edge. Removing ourselves from a place of conflict is essential: an abusive relationship, a war-torn village, a tendency to demean and diminish our own talents. But we must keep going, keep building, keep reminding ourselves that peace is ever expansive. There's the *magis* again, that descent into the vastness of ourselves and our unfolding vocation. Positive peace allows us to make that journey.

There are forces at work in our world that would have us settle for negative peace, that would manipulate a state of negative peace as an opportunity to do insidious violence. Look again at Barbie. She was not actually being attacked. The casual viewer would say that the scene was one of peace, but Barbie *felt* that violence lurked just beneath the surface. This is an essential insight about structural violence.

Structural violence, Galtung tells us, creates "settings within which individuals may do enormous amounts of harm to other human beings without ever intending to do so, just performing their regular duties as a job defined in the structure."[4] Climate change is an obvious example: How much harm do we do to one another simply by catching a flight? By eating an inordinate amount of meat? By purchasing shampoo and conditioner in plastic bottles? These are just mundane activities that many of us participate in without much reflection.

And that's the point: The structure of our society is built this way. There are some places we can't easily get to without flying, even though each flight demands a tremendous amount of fuel that then further erodes our climate. Some of my family's traditional, most beloved meals include beef, but we hardly think of the expansion of livestock pasture at the expense of ancient forests. And I have to wash my hair! There are so few places where I can fill up an empty plastic bottle with new hair product—and that's if I even have an empty bottle on hand.

These are simple tasks to simply live, but how devastating, how violent they are, when observed at scale. The flight I take is just *one* flight; I've only bought *one* ticket. But how many tickets are purchased a day? How many planes take off as a result? How much fuel is used to keep those planes in the air—and what are the consequences for the climate? It's true—I can't easily get to Europe without getting on a plane. So, I buy a plane ticket. In so doing, I incentivize more planes and the purchase of more tickets, and the cycle continues. There's little I can do on my own to disincentivize this ongoing pollution, and I have to get to Europe, after all. So I do nothing; I carry on as I always have.

But taken to scale, the results are overwhelming: rising seas and changing weather patterns that wash homes away and destroy crops needed to sustain the global food supply. With less food and less land, communities are forced to fight simply to survive. Those fights can and do become deadly. Did I cause this by purchasing that flight overseas? Perhaps not. But I did contribute to the system that caused it. Why did I do that? I'm a decent guy—but there are no obvious and accessible means to resist this system on my own. The violence is baked into the system.

This brings us to another important concept: cultural violence. Cultural violence, Galtung says, can make "structural violence look, even feel, right—or at least not wrong."[5] We say, "That's just the way it's done." "That's just the place of women in society." "That's just how we treat LGBTQ+ people." "That's just how the climate is." Structural violence becomes upheld by the very people it seeks to harm. Think of that plane ticket: I want to live on this planet, and I want my children and grandchildren to as well. But that small, trivial purchase, when seen in this way, actually acts against my own interests.

Very often, we don't even realize that we're caught up in this mess. Think of other instances of structural injustice. If asked, we'd say, "Of course we don't support racist policies!" But the structures do. "Of course we don't believe women are less than men!" But our pay scale seems to suggest otherwise. And so on.

Here's the problem: In instances of negative peace, structural violence can run rampant. I remember the first time I was introduced to this concept, this idea that our society is threaded by violence. I disagreed. Then I was encouraged to think about a library. What happens if you make too much noise? The librarian gives you a stern look and makes a hushing sound, right? What if you keep doing it? The cycle repeats itself until eventually you're asked to leave. What if you refuse to leave and instead carry on as you've been? I imagine that weary librarian might call some sort of law enforcement to escort you from the premises. And if you put up a fight? I don't think it's too hard to imagine that you might end up restrained, maybe even locked up for a brief stint. And so on.

That's the ultimate threat, right? If common human decency doesn't keep you quiet at the library, then I imagine this lurking threat of violence might, this notion that you will be removed from society all together, if even just for a moment. After all, what made you listen to law enforcement? Was it their stern looks? That didn't work for the librarian. Perhaps it was the firearm on their hip or the Taser in their hand.

This may be a silly example, but I wonder if there are many places in our lives that don't have this shadow of violence. This notion that if we step out of line, if we don't go along with societal expectations—both good and bad—we'll face some serious repercussions. For me in that library, I quiet down. But for Barbie—and for countless *real* women—acquiescence to societal norms means not pushing back on clear moments of misogyny. Violence is always a threat. Is this logic at least in part responsible for why we still live in a decaying climate, in a society often unraveled by racism, sexism, colonialism, and all the rest? Violence continues because standing up to violence is scary and ferreting out its roots is hard.

But if we settle for "No one is getting shot at," the bar for peace is quite low indeed. True peace demands that we not only put down our weapons but also imagine new ways of living together that allow for the full human flourishing of every member of our human family and all creation. Structural peace, Galtung and MacQueen remind us, requires equity, reciprocity, integration, holism, and inclusion. "This is what friendship, close kinship and neighborship, a good family and a good married couple, good relations of worship and workship, are about. . . . At the macro-level this points to a community, even a union, of countries. And at the mega-level to . . . a joint project of human dignity for all. As a bulwark, an immune system against violence."[6]

Standards over Structures

How might Ignatian spirituality help us navigate these treacherous waters? We have to shine light on these sinister forces of violence if we are ever to eliminate them. The Two Standards Meditation, from the previous chapter, is one of the most powerful Ignatian tools to help us differentiate evil from good.

Recall that the standard of the enemy is demarcated by a three-step progression: attachment to ever more riches, a perverted quest for increased praise and honor, and finally, an obsession with self—a bloated, swollen pride that is unable to even recognize the needs or inherent dignity of others. The standard of the enemy is one that draws our attention increasingly to ourselves, to what we lack and to ways in which we might instead exert power over others. The enemy wants us to stand on a lonely island, obsessed with defending ourselves and our stuff and blind to any communal responsibility. Who has time to help or care about others when I'm so busy looking out for my own self-interests?

Father Dean Brackley notes that the standard of the enemy is best summarized by the idea of "upward mobility"—the clear opposite of the "downward mobility" we discussed in a previous chapter. Brackley writes:

> The principal life strategy is "upward mobility" toward the goal of "success." While some can never rise high enough on the slippery ladder, others can rest content with a modicum of security. But no individual can change the rules of the game. Even when they act with good will, upwardly mobile individuals participate in wider, ambiguous processes. The logic of the ladder fuels the kind of competition that undermines trust and community. From my slippery rung, I perceive the climber below me as a threat.[7]

Trapped in these systems, it's all we can do to keep climbing, keep looking out for our own interests and *maybe* those of our closest circles.

And why? Because we don't want to find ourselves cast down to the bottom of the ladder. We don't want to find ourselves the victim of these systems in which we live and work, so we pursue more and more wealth to protect our livelihood; we pursue more and more honors to protect our social standing; we inflate our pride to convince ourselves that the dark side of these social structures couldn't ever actually affect *us*. We're much too important. We're not like *them*—whoever they happen to be.

In so doing, in accidentally stumbling down the path of the enemy's standard, we uphold the systems that do violence all around us *because we personally and momentarily benefit*. Racism, sexism, colonialism, homophobia—in each of these forms of structural violence and any other that might come to mind, one group of people desperately scrambles up that slippery ladder in the hopes that they won't be found at the bottom. Rather than come together to reject the system, we unknowingly allow the system to divide us so that we see one another as a threat.

Brackley says we should use the image of a pyramid; there can only be an ever-smaller number of people at the top of "success" (the tip of the pyramid) and an ever-greater number of people at the bottom. "In the pyramid, authority and power, which are necessary in social life, are exercised as domination, to contain weaker groups and keep them dependent, ignorant and divided," Brackley says. "The pyramid logic generates corruptions and provokes hostile reactions but, above all, a climate of fear, mistrust and coercion."[8]

This standard of the enemy becomes systematized in this way: "Systemic unfairness and corruption requires systematic cover-up—which is partly engineered and partly taken for granted as 'common sense.'"[9] Challenging that common sense becomes increasingly difficult—we might say this is participation in cultural violence. Failure to challenge that common sense ensures that structural violence continues.

So what should we do? Go in the opposite direction; pursue the downward mobility of Christ. Call to mind the standard of Christ: guideposts of poverty, rejection, and humility. For Brackley, "solidarity is the social meaning of humility." The pursuit of the downward mobility of Christ "means entering the world of the poor, assuming their cause and, to some degree, their condition." Brackley is clear to stress that each of our lives and vocations necessarily manifest solidarity differently. "Solidarity doesn't mean destitution. It has nothing to do with denying our training or neglecting our talents" or obligations.[10] As we reflected in the proceeding chapter, the standards are about setting our lives on a certain trajectory.

To that end, "we will feel uncomfortable with superfluities when poor friends lack essentials. Attachments to them (our friends) will detach us from luxuries, and even necessities."[11] This desire to stand *with* others—with *everyone*—will help

115

us break free from that lonely island where the enemy wishes to strand us. In practice, this might not mean physically placing yourself in a refugee camp, for example—though it might. Rather, this desire should shape how you set up your life and how you react to the people you find within it. You may not travel to a refugee settlement, but you might volunteer at a shelter, give money to an organization that supports refugees, or simply ensure you're keeping up with the news. The standard of Christ is a weaving together of all people, all creation, and an awakening to the real needs, experiences, passions, and desires of each person and to the needs of creation. We are constantly called to prepare our hearts and minds to respond to Christ's invitation whenever and wherever it comes.

By endeavoring to better see, to better understand the lives of others rather than blindly scampering up the ladder of upward mobility, we can see more clearly the roots of structural violence and the social systems in place from which we desperately desire liberation. As the great theologian Gustavo Gutiérrez writes, "A spirituality of liberation will center on a *conversion* to the neighbor, the oppressed person, the exploited social class, the despised ethnic group, the dominated country. . . . Conversion means a radical transformation of ourselves; it means thinking, feeling, and living as Christ—present in exploited and alienated persons."[12]

We All Lose

I used to work in downtown Baltimore. My colleagues and I frequently wandered down Howard Street in search of coffee—there was a Starbucks about a ten-minute walk from our office.

Howard is a busy street. The light rail passes directly through it, and right near the office were two light rail stops. There was car traffic too—a lot of it—and we were only a block or two away from Lexington Market, a huge indoor and rather famous marketplace. All this is to say, the street was busy; lots of people were always around.

I probably walked that route every day; I drink a lot of coffee. And I rarely walked alone; a colleague or two always joined me. We'd talk, brainstorm, and vent. Although the streets were busy, my little cohort always kept to itself.

One particular day stands out in my memory. Our coffee expedition consisted of me and maybe five colleagues, all of them women. I was a few steps behind that day—probably on my phone—so my colleagues rounded the corner onto Howard Street before me.

Even several paces back and distracted, I could not miss the catcalling, the whistling, the names. A group of men across the street had decided it was their right to harass my colleagues right there on the street. I was shocked. How many times had I made this journey, and never had I experienced something like this!

I caught up to my colleagues, aghast. They were irritated but unsurprised. "Happens all the time, Eric," they said. "Like every day. Just not when you're around."

Of course. The dynamics are different when I'm around—and not because I'm big or intimidating. But I am another guy.

I mentioned it to my wife that night, sharing with her my shock and disgust. She shook her head. "Of course, Eric. Happens to me too."

I doubt I need to belabor the point. It's an all-too-common version of the scene from *Barbie*. The fact that it happened—*happens*—is disconcerting enough, but that day and for many days since, I've been struck by how my presence affected the course of events: When I was with my colleagues, those guys on the other side of the street stayed quiet; when I was absent, those guys got loud.

No one should need an escort in order to be treated with the bare minimum of respect. But what this instance made clear to me was that the tendency to violence is there all the time. It's just a matter of whether or not it reveals itself, whether or not people feel as though they have "permission" to act on what our society calls "common sense." Remember the "undertone of violence" Barbie felt getting ogled by strangers? Just as Ken failed to see it, so too was I unable to see it. My colleagues, however, were painfully aware of it whether or not I was present. The point is that *it's there all the same*. How can we all see those undertones more clearly—of patriarchy, racism, colonialism, and so on—and root them out from our society?

On another day in another place, I got into the car of a ridesharing service, headed to the airport. The driver turned to me and began telling me about his girlfriend. I made casual eye contact, nodded politely, and interjected at appropriate points. He began describing her in a bit too much detail. Then he started talking about the time he was in Rio, telling me about all the beautiful women he wanted to dance with, get with, and so on. Lots of details. I continued to nod politely, though gave very little in response. I tried to change the conversation.

I sat in the back of that car wondering what it was about me that gave the impression I wanted to hear about this guy's sexual exploits. I didn't want to hear details about his girlfriend or about the women he was apparently cheating on her with. I didn't want to commiserate about how "we men" just want to get with all sorts of women, or how "we men" feel tied down by relationships. It was a long car ride.

Clearly, the driver knew nothing about me—save for my name and destination—but he assumed that since I was also a man, I'd want to swap stories of women, that I'd applaud his adventures and pity his newly tied-down lifestyle. I didn't and I don't, and I was left feeling more than a bit unsettled by the "group" I was being cast into—that's not the kind of guy I am, and I wouldn't want anyone to think so. Certainly not my two daughters, not my wife, not my mother. You get my point.

When caught in these systems of violence, we need to liberate not just the victim but also the oppressor. To break a system, you have to completely transform the relationships therein. "A political injustice not only wounds its victim, but can also, like a discharging cannon, recoil back to wound the perpetrator," writes Daniel Philpott, associate professor of political science and peace studies at the University of Notre Dame. "That evil injures the soul of the wrongdoer, often manifested in severe psychological damage."[13] We certainly don't favor the oppressor over the victim, but we do name the fact that such encompassing violence does damage to all parties. True liberation liberates all, and that must be our goal—because true and lasting peace requires the participation of all parties.

I think of that rideshare driver—his relationship to the women in his life was certainly not a healthy one, even if he did benefit as a man from the hidden workings of patriarchy. And I certainly didn't appreciate being lumped in as someone who would find his exploits relatable. Can we imagine a way forward where he and I are also liberated from the injustices of patriarchy?

Rules for Discernment

I'd like to propose one more Ignatian approach to unraveling structural violence. Ironically, I turn to Ignatius's Rules for Discernment, which are riddled with the language of patriarchy. For example, "The enemy conducts himself as a woman. He is a weakling before a show of strength."[14] It can be hard to see the spiritual forest for all the sexist trees here, but again, we turn to Galtung and MacQueen, who encourage a "responsible reinterpretation of a passage that seems to promote war or violence"—or in this case, misogyny.[15]

Ignatius gives us three rules, which I excerpt below:

1. "The enemy becomes weak, loses courage, and turns to flight with his seductions as soon as one leading a spiritual life faces his temptations boldly, and does exactly the opposite of what he suggests."[16]

2. "The enemy of our human nature tempts a just soul with his wiles and seductions [and] desires that they be received secretly and kept secret."[17]

3. Comparing the enemy to a commander laying siege to a castle, Ignatius says, "The enemy of our human nature investigates from every side all our virtues. . . . Where he finds the defense . . . weakest and most deficient, there he attacks."[18]

The enemy desires that we fail to stand up for what we know to be right and just, that we allow evil to grow in secrecy and shadow, and that we pay little attention to our own weaknesses and shortcomings.

How do these reflections factor into structural violence? We've already seen that structural injustice persists because we accept it as "common sense." We ignore the "undertones of violence" because either we ourselves are not personally or immediately affected or we simply do not see clearly the truth of the matter. Even if we do see clearly, we are tepid in our response to such injustice because we ourselves are benefiting in some way.

I think about my time in that car. I knew what the driver was saying was inappropriate, but instead of responding boldly, of naming it and encouraging the conversation to go elsewhere, I sat back quietly, hoping he might just knock it off.

Taking Ignatius's rules in reverse, once we identify ourselves as trapped in an upwardly mobile system—one that does violence in hidden, unseen ways—we take action. First, we examine ourselves: Where are we most vulnerable to the system's workings? Where are we most likely to benefit in subtle ways that might encourage us to turn a blind eye? For me, I could easily sit in that car or walk down that street and simply put my head down. How tempting to go along to get along and remain in comfort.

Second, we consider what shadows are concealing the system's true ends. How can we work for transparency? Whose eyes do we need to open—and how can we do so in a way that is effective but also charitable? I think about that driver: If I had been forceful and insulting, making him feel uncomfortable, I would've certainly fallen on the right side of justice. But I wonder if I would've helped him to see the violence being done in his name. I wonder if I would have actually advanced the cause of peace.

All the same, Ignatius's final rule is one of boldness: We can't back down from the cause of peace. We have to stand up for what is right, plainly naming those systems and structures that reinforce structural or cultural violence.

We can't ignore the undertones.

A Spiritual Exercise for Peace Work

Opening Prayer

Pray for the grace to discover clear and consistent means through which you can actively help unravel systems of structural and cultural violence.

Prayer Text

Then the scribes and the Pharisees brought a woman who had been caught in adultery and made her stand in the middle. They said to him, "Teacher, this woman was caught in the very act of committing adultery. Now in the law, Moses commanded us to stone such women. So what do you say?" They said this to test him, so that they could have some charge to bring against him. Jesus bent down and began to write on the ground with his finger. But when they continued asking him, he straightened up and said to them, "Let the one among you who is without sin be the first to throw a stone at her." Again he bent down and wrote on the ground. And in response, they went away one by one, beginning with the elders. So he was left alone with the woman before him. Then Jesus straightened up and said to her, "Woman, where are they? Has no one condemned you?" She replied, "No one, sir." Then Jesus said, "Neither do I condemn you. Go, [and] from now on do not sin any more."

John 8:3–11

Reflection Exercises

- In the passage above, the crowd goes along with a perverse act of violence because that's *just the way things are*—a clear and disconcerting example of cultural and structural violence. Jesus steps in and challenges the group to imagine a new way forward; he disrupts the cycle of violence. How is Jesus inviting you to follow his example?
- Who are the people in your community who are victims of similar violence done to the woman in the Scripture passage? Is the violence obvious—as in the passage—or more subtle? How can you help bring such violence to light?

Conversation

- In conversation with God or with neighbor, reflect on how you or your community have been victims of cultural or structural violence. How did you know? What did it feel like? How did you go about revealing this violence to others?

- Now, in conversation with God or with neighbor, reflect on how you or your community have been perpetrators of cultural or structural violence. How did you know? What did it feel like? What comes next after this uncomfortable discovery?

Journal

- Spend time with the three Ignatian steps to uncovering structural violence: Recognize and name personal blind spots, be honest and transparent, and speak boldly. How can you integrate these steps into your own life? Note places where they might be particularly helpful.

CHAPTER 8

Embracing a Spirit of Indifference

I like to tell myself I live simply, humbly, and intentionally. I only have what I need, and what I have I make good use of for myself and those around me.

Then my wife asks me to go through my closet, to donate old, unused clothes, and the facade crumbles. I still have dress shirts from when I was in high school—shirts that clearly and cruelly no longer fit. Simple living, indeed.

"But they might come back in style!" I protest. "Then I'd just have to buy them all over again. I'm really saving money—living *super* simply."

My wife rolls her eyes and kindly says nothing about any guts or waistlines that may have expanded beyond the scope of the shirts in question in the past twenty years.

What else do I find when I go through my closet? Not just clothes from high school, but clothes that have some sentimental significance—a gift from a grandparent or a memorable, funny tie that shouldn't be seen in public. These are things I'm loath to part with but equally reluctant to put on and wear in real life. I open some drawers and find a sock that I love but whose partner has long been lost. I keep it, I tell myself, because I could always mix and match with other solo socks. I never actually do. I have shoes that are nice, arguably still in style, but that I've worn no more than a half dozen times over as many years. But the day might yet come . . .

I'm attached to these things. Not in a terribly unhealthy way: Everything fits nicely in the requisite closet, drawers, and shelving. If the house caught fire, I'd certainly save the children first and then the cat. I'd give these old pieces of clothing barely a thought.

But still, these things take up space—literal and mental. They cause me to pause when I'm asked to part with them. While the nostalgia and the memories are good, they, too, clutter my mind, distracting from the present. The past does not need to cling to the present by way of one battered sock.

Think on your own life, your own burgeoning closets. What's in them? Only that which is necessary? More importantly, what hold over you do these things have? Can you part with them? Or, like me, do you only imagine parting with them due to an act of God?

Ignatian spirituality anticipates this very predicament. In this chapter, we'll explore the meditation that helps us see our way through it—from inordinate attachment to inner peace.

Three Types of People

Imagine you've acquired ten thousand ducats. Unsure what a ducat is? Me too. (Ignatius of Loyola, you'll recall, lived and wrote in Spain in the early sixteenth century.)

Let's start again. I don't think Ignatius will mind if we imagine instead that we've acquired ten thousand dollars, or an equally large sum of money in the currency of your choosing.

No foul play was afoot; no one was beaten, robbed, or murdered for us to come into this bit of wealth.

All the same, as Ignatius says, that sum of money weighs on our minds. Now that we have it, we're loath to part with it. We think on all the possibilities now available to us: the fancy clothes and friends and travel and charitable donations. What will *we* do with this money? What will it do *for us*?

This sum, we discover, has control over us, over our present and future. As Ignatius says, we are not indifferent to the money and all it means. Instead, we hold on to our options tightly, reluctant to surrender any and anxious about them all. Because we worry about a future that has not yet arrived, we fail to live in the present. We fail to make ourselves available to whatever needs may arise now.

So Ignatius writes, we wish to "find peace in God our Lord by ridding [ourselves] of the burden arising from the attachment to the sum acquired."[1] How do we do this? How do we think about this attachment and our hoped-for indifference? (In the Ignatian tradition, indifference does not mean apathy; rather, it points to radical availability to whatever path God desires for us. More on that below.)

In the Second Week of the Spiritual Exercises, Ignatius introduces a meditation called the Three Classes of People. They've come into the wealth described above—all the ducats!—but earnestly wish to find peace and live as God desires, letting go of the monetary attachment by which they find themselves burdened. What happens next?

The first type of person procrastinates. They twiddle their thumbs and clasp their hands together and stare at the pile of cash. They want to become indifferent; they *wish* they didn't give this large sum of money so much of their time and attention. Then they die, having never acted, never having decided. Inner peace proves elusive.

The second type of person pretends to rid themselves of this attachment. They tell God that they're ready and willing—ready and willing for God to come around to their side of things. They don't desire the will of God; they desire that God conform to their will. Rather than truly release control over the sum, they cling to it and hope that God blesses the decision. This isn't indifference; this is a facade, akin to keeping all those high school shirts because they might come back into fashion. Attachment masquerades as simple living. There's no peace here, either—we're still riddled by doubt and fear of loss.

The third and final type of person starts at the same place as the second: They've decided to rid themselves of this attachment. But they don't simply flush the money; they don't just give the lump sum to the nearest charity. Ridding oneself of the sum simply to *rid oneself of the sum* isn't any better an approach when dealing with attachment. The attachment still holds sway, it's just now we're attached to the idea of *not being attached*. How does the third person riddle their way out?

They "want to rid themselves of the attachment, but they wish to do so in such a way that they desire neither to retain nor to relinquish the sum acquired. They seek only to will and not will as God . . . inspires."[2] They seek to be truly *indifferent*.

Whether or not our inner peace is threatened by money or pride or some other inordinate attachment, the solution isn't about letting go of things just to let go of them. Rather, it's about not holding so tightly that we fail to let God in, that we fail to let God be God. It's about loosening our grip so that we allow God to call us into who we are meant to be.

Peace is found in that place—the lightly held inner sanctum in which we hear the affirming voice of God delighting in us now and dreaming up what we might still become. Peace is experienced in the dance that ensues.

Loosely Held Words

When I submitted the manuscript for my first book, my editor—as is the way of editors—responded with edits. And I—as is the way of writers—immediately bristled at imagined offense to my writing.

Doesn't he know this book is perfect? I've poured my soul into this! There's nothing to be improved upon!

I was too attached to what was, to the static status quo of my written words.

The writing process demands edits. It is the rare writer who actually gets it perfect out of the gate. And it's the good editor who can pull from this writer the insightful gems that are buried in the muck of muddled writing.

This is the feedback I received: The stories I'd written, the anecdotes I'd shared, were too focused on *me*. For the kind of book I was purporting to write—for the spiritual writing I was claiming to do—I'd need to turn *I* into *you*. I needed to invite the reader in, give them space to see themselves, and shine the light less on me and more on *us*.

Why was that? In this specific case, the book I was writing was meant to be helpful to other people; I wasn't writing a memoir. At a more general level, I needed to let go of how I saw my stories and instead allow them to serve others. I needed to loosen my grip, stop squeezing meaning from my words, and instead let them flutter about, beckoning others along their own journey.

I needed to cultivate a bit of indifference.

Faith, Not Certainty

Indifference sounds like a cruel word, embodying a lack of caring, even coldness, but in the Ignatian tradition, indifference is an *availability*. It's not that we don't care about the needs of our world but that we want to be available to respond to those needs as is most appropriate to our own context. We want to embody and live out of our own *magis*—which necessarily means letting go of those things that hold us back, things that we may even believe to be good and useful. This may even mean letting go of dreams about who we might yet become so as to be the person God needs us now to be. (Think back to chapter 1 and my anxious social media scrolling in a hospital room.)

We've already reflected on the importance of *magis* to our own inner peace, to finding and rejoicing in our own unique purpose. Indifference—and this meditation on the three types of people—helps us formulate a certain kind of disposition toward peace that takes things a step further.

A college friend of mine once said something to the effect of, "To have faith is to always be open to being completely wrong." I immediately disagreed, but my friend persisted—and his words have stuck with me more than a decade later.

Does a life of faith require a willingness to be wrong? Isn't that the *antithesis* of a life of faith?

A Jesuit friend of mine once said something similar to what my college friend said: "The opposite of faith isn't doubt; it's certainty." Therein lies our peace-seeking disposition. Faith and the spiritual life demand that we let God be God. We throw ourselves into the fog of the world and muddle through as best we can. We can't see everything—past, future, even present. At times, we can barely see what's right in front of us. As we let God be God, we will discover a God of surprises beyond our wildest imaginings. How tempting it is to put that same God in a box!

If we allow our spirituality to permeate all we do, including our quest for peace, then we find that our grip loosens rather than tightens. This disposition of indifference doesn't mean that nothing matters or that we don't live out of our beliefs. Rather, the challenge here is to cultivate a spirituality of curiosity, an availability to be surprised. We seek to learn new things from new perspectives, contributing ever more to the mosaic of human experience.

People have unique experiences, insights, hopes, and dreams. We all come from different places and contexts. We see the world in different ways. That's okay. We are who we are—but we look to others in all that *they* are too. We let other people discover and become their authentic selves, while remembering that we live on the same planet and are ultimately dependent on one another. Together, we move forward. Together, we build.

Differences can be difficult. Compromise is necessary. Here we begin to see how peace fits into the puzzle—or doesn't. Think of the ideological frames with which so many of us view the world. These frames come to us from culture and economics, religion and politics. (Remember those instances of cultural and structural violence?) They can be as simple as family traditions (*this is the only way to prepare a meatloaf*) to traditions of higher stakes (*we must raise our children with this particular faith*). It's not hard to extrapolate how these individual ways of living, these even mundane frames, can explode into conflict and violence.

Let's turn to Ignatian indifference and ask how we ourselves are attached to these ideologies, frames, and ways of proceeding. Do we cling in certainty, refusing to ever give an inch? Or do we allow space to get things wrong now and again, space in which we might be surprised by our God of surprises?

If we try to embody that third type of person, perhaps we can begin to see how each of us can live out of our own unique beliefs and context, while also allowing the God of the universe to work, free from our constraints. When we free God, we also free ourselves. We allow God to be God and *God to be God in and through us.*

I am not suggesting we surrender important traditions or abandon principled beliefs. But I do wonder how we can ever fully engage with those who are different from us if we refuse to entertain the notion that a different perspective may have merit and may reflect a lived experience as true and valuable as our own. Perhaps a degree of humility is needed to wade into the uncertain waters of dialogue. We want to begin developing relationships through honest conversation; we don't want to turn our backs on our fellow human beings in a disposition of contempt and dismissal. One path leads to the standard of Christ, where humility births possibility. The other leads to the standard of the enemy, where pride begets isolation.

Clinging to certainty doesn't allow for the kind of response that I believe Christ desires. Rather, it makes us rigid, our hands clasped too tightly to that which we don't want to give up. We waste time trying to prove ourselves completely and absolutely correct rather than responding to the lived reality of another person. As a result, violence, mistrust, and judgment flourish under our noses.

Remember the first kind of person with their lump sum of money—the one who did nothing but procrastinate? That person failed to act, so enchanted were they by the riches that held them fast. We may be inclined to dismiss this person: We all know people who fail to act in a timely manner. They reap the consequences of their inaction! At a macrolevel, we want everyone to reach their fullest potential, to find God's will for their lives, but what does one hypothetical life matter to the rest of us? So-and-so missed out; what does it matter to me? Quite a lot, I think. Let's not think in terms of individual lives; let's think in terms of the disposition that this way of living encourages. Now we might begin to see how this disposition at a macrolevel can have far-reaching consequences.

Think not of sums of money but of intractable conflicts made more difficult by people who refuse to give an inch. It's not simply an individual life that fails to reach its potential; it's entire communities that wither under prolonged warfare.

Think about any number of global conflicts, wars waged between two groups of ideologically opposed combatants. When leaders dig in and refuse to negotiate, refuse to *compromise*, lives are lost. This is not to suggest that all sides in a conflict are equally responsible—of course not, and justice must be dealt accordingly. But when we are trapped in cycles of violence with any prospect of dialogue pushed aside, I wonder if we're not clinging too tightly to past and future ideas while forgetting about the people suffering in the present.

Cultivating indifference reminds us to be curious, to be open, to be available to that which is different, that which is challenging. We turn to others in charity, offering grace rather than venom. We do so not because we want to give up on ourselves and our beliefs; no—rather, we want to *enlarge* our worldview, to tell a bigger story, to try to see how all these pieces might fit together. If we don't, if we insist on enforcing our way over another's through conflict, then we simply perpetuate systems of structural violence.

Indifferent Immersion

During my senior year at Fairfield University, I applied to lead one of the service immersion trips that took place during spring break. There were two trips planned, and the destinations were Nicaragua and Belize. I had been to Nicaragua the previous year as part of a research course, so I was pretty confident Belize was where I was meant to go.

It won't surprise you to learn that I was assigned to lead the group going to Nicaragua.

"But I was just in Nicaragua," I said to the campus minister who was coordinating the trips. "I'd rather go to Belize."

"Take some time," the campus minister replied. "Take it to prayer. If you really believe you need to go to Belize, we can talk about it."

Despite having attended a Jesuit school for nearly four years, I knew very little about Ignatian indifference, but as soon as I voiced my reasons for wanting to go to Belize, I knew I was destined for Nicaragua. Why? The entire purpose of immersing myself in a different culture, of traveling to a different country, of claiming I wanted to do service was to be challenged to let go, to grow, to be pushed outside my comfort zone—and to be present to people, whoever they might be, that I might accompany and learn from. The point of spending a week on such an excursion wasn't to add a new stamp to my passport; it was to make myself *freely available* to a larger community, whether that be fellow students or the Nicaraguans I would meet. Putting my own parameters around the experience seemed to miss the point entirely. If I was truly indifferent to the experience, channeling a desire to *serve* in a way that was healthy, it shouldn't have mattered to me if I was going to Nicaragua, Belize, or New Jersey.

Practicing Ignatian indifference means actively making ourselves available to the will of God in our lives, as well as in the fabric of our society and world. I had done the first part—injecting myself into an experience of service and community—but I had failed miserably at the second. Instead, I needed to change my perspective and priorities. It wasn't about what *I* wanted from the experience; it was about what the *experience* wanted from and for me.

Think, too, for a moment about that campus minister who directed me back to prayer. He could have very easily said, "No, Eric. You're going to Nicaragua. Here's why." Instead, he invited me to reflect on what I wanted in a way that invited curiosity. What he was implying through his words was this: *I wonder what God is saying to Eric. I wonder how God is working in Eric. I wonder what God desires of and for Eric.* He would have been well within his rights to give me concrete instruction; instead, he trusted God at work in me. He made room for our God of surprises, holding all possible outcomes lightly. I wonder how many of our personal and political interactions would end differently if instead of beginning with resolute answers, we instead turned to curiosity, wondering what God was up to in another person's life and prayer.

This is an important reminder for our lives of peace. We hold all things lightly, including expectations of ourselves and of others. We make room for others not solely by engaging in conversation with a disposition of curiosity but also by allowing ourselves to be drawn into places and circumstances that may be unexpected. If our world is shattered by violence, I wonder how effective we can be at bringing about peace if we cling resolutely to the life we've planned for ourselves. Instead, perhaps we allow the Spirit to surprise us, to usher us into new places and new opportunities. To do so, we must once again loosen our grip on what we think we need and be available to what God might be asking of us.

A loose grip—be it on plans, beliefs, opinions, or our own identities—makes us better prepared to reach out and catch the Spirit of peace as it flutters by.

A Spiritual Exercise for Peace Work

Opening Prayer

Pray for the grace to hold all things lightly—and discern those areas of your life to which you cling with unhealthy vigor.

Prayer Text

For God who said, "Let light shine out of darkness," has shone in our hearts to bring to light the knowledge of the glory of God on the face of [Jesus] Christ.

But we hold this treasure in earthen vessels, that the surpassing power may be of God and not from us. We are afflicted in every way, but not constrained; perplexed, but not driven to despair; persecuted, but not abandoned; struck down, but not destroyed; always carrying about in the body the dying of Jesus, so that the life of Jesus may also be manifested in our body. For we who live are constantly being given up to death for the sake of Jesus, so that the life of Jesus may be manifested in our mortal flesh.

So death is at work in us, but life in you. Since, then, we have the same spirit of faith, according to what is written, "I believed, therefore I spoke," we too believe and therefore speak, knowing that the one who raised the Lord Jesus will raise us also with Jesus and place us with you in his presence. Everything indeed is for you, so that the grace bestowed in abundance on more and more people may cause the thanksgiving to overflow for the glory of God.

Therefore, we are not discouraged; rather, although our outer self is wasting away, our inner self is being renewed day by day. For this momentary light affliction is producing for us an eternal weight of glory beyond all comparison, as we look not to what is seen but to what is unseen; for what is seen is transitory, but what is unseen is eternal.

2 Corinthians 4:6–18

Reflection Exercises

- In the Scripture passage, we see the paradox of pursuing God's message of peace and justice. We find ourselves afflicted and yet free to act, despairing and yet hopeful in God's presence, and so on. How might Ignatian indifference help us cultivate a disposition that makes us available to serve God and God's people as God desires?

Conversation

- In the First Principle and Foundation at the beginning of the Spiritual Exercises, Ignatius writes: "We must make ourselves indifferent to all created things, as far as we are allowed free choice and are not under any prohibition. Consequently, as far as we are concerned, we should not prefer health to sickness, riches to poverty, honor to dishonor, a long life to a short life. The same holds for all other things. Our one desire and choice should be what is more conducive to the end for which we are created."[3] In conversation with God or with neighbor, discuss how this passage from the Exercises helps illuminate the prayer text above. How might it lead us to practice peace?

Journal

- Make a list of all the things that are important to you: relationships, professional goals, personal hopes, items, and so on. Spend time reflecting on whether or not you have cultivated a spirit of indifference toward those things. Does something have too much control over you?

CHAPTER 9

The Nonviolent Christ

Since the earliest conception of this book, I knew this chapter would be about nonviolence. It had to be. Nonviolence is foundational to any spirituality of peace. More importantly, the place in which we find ourselves in our journey through the Spiritual Exercises—the Third Week—is where I inevitably bump up against the call to nonviolence.

The Third Week is when Ignatius invites us to contemplate the passion and death of Jesus. We pray for the grace to feel "sorrow, compassion and shame because the Lord is going to his suffering for my sins."[1] Our experience of this week is one of profound agony as we behold Jesus—our friend, our companion, the one whom we walked with through his ministry and his miracles—tortured, betrayed, and killed. We are meant to feel this pain poignantly. After all, how else should we feel when a beloved friend is made to suffer?

And now you rightly say, "Eric, it sounds like this week is actually the most violent of the weeks. How is it that you've concluded that you must write about nonviolence?" It's true. During the Third Week's meditations, we face the violence embedded in our tradition. Christianity inevitably arrives at this point of violence done to our God, to the innocent. In the Catholic tradition, the crucifix hangs prominently in our churches so as to remind us of this intense suffering, of this God who suffered *for* and *with* us. An encounter with violence—with the violence of our world, the violence embedded in our systems, even within our very selves—is inevitable for a person desiring to work for peace. We've already reflected on this.

So why turn to nonviolence?

Many years ago, my wife was the young adult minister at our parish. One of the annual initiatives she organized was the Lenten book club. The most impactful of the books we read as a community was John Dear's *Walking the Way: Following Jesus on the Lenten Journey of Gospel Nonviolence to the Cross and Resurrection.* The book struck a nerve in the best way. Our band of twenty-somethings gathered each week of Lent to grapple with the violence done to our neighbors, to our communities, to our world by systems of injustice. We were challenged to see Jesus's road to Calvary in a totally new way. I'll talk more about that as this chapter goes on.

But the thing I remember the most is how we joked about Dear's frequent—near incessant—use of the phrase "the non-violent Jesus" or "the nonviolent Christ." Again and again we read those words and we'd laugh. "I think we got the message!" we'd say each week. "Perhaps we need a different turn of phrase!"

But you know what? I can't *not* hear that phrase now. I can't look at Jesus's own grappling with systemic injustice as anything but nonviolent—and that's in large part due to Dear's book and our faith sharing. My own spiritual director often commented on how timely that book selection was, how important it seemed for my own faith journey. The nonviolent Jesus is the only Jesus I know.

The word *nonviolent* carries with it a tremendous amount of gravitas. It calls to my mind heroes of nonviolence that I grew up learning about or hearing mentioned in a litany of impressive people: Óscar Romero, Dorothy Day, Martin Luther King Jr., Rosa Parks, Mahatma Gandhi.

Here's my confession: Though I knew that the Third Week of the Exercises would demand I address nonviolence, I have dreaded writing this chapter. Why? Because I am no hero of nonviolence. A voice whispers in my ear telling me that I have no experience; I have no right to write about such an awe-inspiring topic. I'm not courageous or brave enough to do the hard work of nonviolence, so how dare I try to write about it!

I am not enough.

Right then, when I realized that there was an insidious voice insisting I wasn't good enough to reflect on this important topic, I found my way in. That voice, I believe, is not of God. If nonviolence is God's preferred path, then anything that insists I'm not up to the challenge must be other-than-God. To again use Ignatius's phrase, that insidious voice is the enemy of our human nature, pushing us away from God's dream for us and from our identity as God's beloved. (Any voice that insists we're not enough cannot possibly be of God.)

How useful for the enemy to convince us that we can't possibly live up to the nonviolent legacy that is ours to claim! How easy, then, it becomes for the enemy to insist instead that we sit at home and ignore the call, that we shrug at the seemingly inevitable cascade of violence and war and suffering. We lock ourselves away in our castle of not-enoughness and watch a world of pain pass us by.

That can't be our way. Rather, we return to our fundamental identity as the beloved of God. We recall that our own *magis* insists we are enough *now* and that God still dreams of all that we may yet become. John Dear, at the beginning of his book *The Nonviolent Life*, says it so well: "Being a person of nonviolence means first of all being nonviolent to ourselves. . . . Practicing nonviolence means claiming our fundamental identity as the beloved sons and daughters of the God of peace, and thus, going forth into the world of war as peacemakers to love every other human being."[2]

This chapter will reflect on the passion of Jesus—the Third Week of the Exercises—and it will be a meditation on the call of nonviolence. Most of all, in this chapter we will reflect together on what it means to be nonviolent toward ourselves so as to then be able to go out to be the face of peace toward others.

The Logic of Nonviolence

The term *nonviolence* may be one we think we instinctively understand: It's being *not* violent, avoiding violence, not harming others, and so on, right? Well, sort of.

"We understand *active nonviolence* as a spirituality, a way of life, a positive and powerful force for social change, and a means of building a more just, peaceful and sustainable global community," writes Marie Dennis, copresident of Pax Christi International in the introduction to the book *Choosing Peace*. "Active nonviolence is a method for challenging and transforming the innumerable forms of direct, cultural, structural and systemic violence; a path for resolving interpersonal, social and international conflict; and a way to protect the vulnerable without resort to violence or lethal force."[3] It's important to recognize, then, that nonviolence isn't just the absence of something; it's not passive. It's an active project that envisions and builds a new, better world. Any true and lasting peace requires active engagement from all parties to both build and sustain.

Pope Francis, in his 2017 World Day of Peace message, underlines this common misconception: "Nonviolence is sometimes taken to mean surrender, lack of involvement and passivity, but this is not the case." He goes on to insist that "the decisive and consistent practice of nonviolence has produced impressive results," and then points to the work of Mother Teresa of

Calcutta, Mahatma Gandhi, and Khan Abdul Ghaffar Khan—all three of whom had a profound impact on Indian life and culture—Martin Luther King Jr., who helped transform civil rights in the United States; and Leymah Gbowee, who, with thousands of other Liberian women, organized nonviolent protests that contributed to the end of the Second Liberian Civil War.[4]

Marie Dennis points to Jesus's own practice of nonviolence: "Neither passive nor weak, Jesus's nonviolence was the power of love in action. In vision and deed, he is the revelation and embodiment of the Nonviolent God, a truth especially illuminated in the Cross and Resurrection."[5] We begin to see the direct connection to the Third Week of the Exercises. In an essay titled "An Overview of Gospel Nonviolence in the Christian Tradition," Ken Butigan and John Dear note how "Christians in many parts of the world have come to see that this word [nonviolence] effectively characterizes Jesus's way—a way that combines *both* an unmistakable rejection of violence *and* the power of love and truth in action for justice, peace and integrity of creation."[6] Let us not forget that Jesus's way is that of downward mobility and goes *through* the cross.

"At some point, all of us who claim to be followers of this person [Jesus] need to change direction and set off with him toward the center of government, empire and religion, with the announcement of God's nonviolent kingdom at hand," writes Dear. "Jesus is going to confront the world of systemic injustice head on, and he's taking us with him."[7]

One year I attended the annual Ignatian Family Teach-in for Justice (IFTJ), an enormous social justice conference for young people in Washington, DC, organized by the Ignatian Solidarity Network. I remember one of the keynote speakers talking about injustice and crucifixion and lived theology. I must have been lost in my own thoughts because I remember very little of the talk itself. But all of a sudden, the speaker said something that caught my attention: "We often reflect on the question, Why did Jesus die?" The speaker went on to say that Jesus died to save us from our sins, to redeem the world, and so on. "But we often miss an essential second question that goes hand in hand with the first," the speaker said. "*Why was Jesus killed?*"

I was floored. I knew in that moment, years ago, that these framing questions would stay with me, that they were important. *Why did Jesus die? Why was Jesus killed?* They sound similar, and yet the differences are profound. The first question has a theological answer, the second, a political one. Jesus was killed because he lived out a way of life that upset the status quo, a way of life that was inclusive and compassionate and, importantly, nonviolent. His way of living caught the powers that be in their own hypocrisy and was consequently deemed threatening. Jesus and this "new" way of life—this so-called good news—needed to be assimilated or destroyed. And Jesus, we know, never goes along to get along.

This, in many ways, is the goal of nonviolence: It draws violence out of our systems and structures like poison from a wound. Jesus's life and legacy revealed the structural and cultural violence lurking in the systems of his time. A God who was inclusive? Who loved the Samaritans? Who blessed the meek and the poor? This was a God who was threatening.

When the legendary civil rights leader John Lewis died, I had the opportunity to write about and reflect on his legacy of nonviolence. My wife and I had listened to several podcasts about Lewis and his fateful stand on the Edmund Pettus Bridge, and we were struck by what we hadn't learned, hadn't *seen*, in high school.

"My wife and I were familiar with these images, as tragic as they are," I wrote. "We knew Martin Luther King Jr. preached nonviolence; we'd seen Black bodies beaten in the streets. What is so often missed, though, in this chapter of high school textbooks is that drawing out violence is precisely the point of nonviolence.

The weapons of nonviolence are the weapons of the oppressor. Standing firmly, peacefully, against injustice ultimately pulls away the curtain on the violent regime that keeps injustice in place."[8] Nonviolence necessarily reveals the violence embedded in our structures. The system, when threatened by a new way of living, needs to respond—and respond forcefully—to any threat to the status quo. Whether on a bridge in Alabama or a cross on Calvary, tenacious nonviolence makes us face a harsh truth: Do we want to live in a society that is held together by war and greed and viciousness—the enemy's standard, if ever I've seen it—or do we want to name these evils that have crept into our daily lives and ferret them out—as we noted in chapter 7? Ultimately, this makes us face an even harsher truth: Our society is divided between those who have the power to do violence and those who do not. Division is not of God; division leads to othering, to hate, to dehumanization, to violence. When we throw down our weapons—throw down our power—we stand alongside those without power in solidarity. We give up our *power over* and instead simply *stand with*.

It's not easy. Nonviolence is uncomfortable because it puts us at risk, but it also puts the whole system at risk. Nonviolence is revolutionary because it raises the question: Can we build something better than this? Can we imagine a way of being that does not harm our neighbors or creation?

That's ultimately what Jesus points to on the cross: our God who dies for us, with us, rather than fighting back. "Put your sword back into its sheath," we again hear Jesus tell those who would defend him. "All who take the sword will perish by the sword" (Matt. 26:52). So, too, with us.

Seeing the Violence of the Cross

The enemy divides, but Christ unites, and Christ's standard is one that points toward an ever more inclusive community.

That's a key point of both the Third and Fourth Weeks of the Exercises.

John English has this to say on the topic: "The Third and Fourth Weeks, taken together may be considered the 'unitive way,' for the grace being sought is union with Christ, first in suffering and then in glory. The unitive way is the stage in our spiritual life when we move out of ourselves toward Christ in much the same way Jesus moved out of himself all through the Passion. Jesus gives himself for others; he forgets himself."[9]

I'm deeply struck by this idea, this image. The meditation on the passion is not simply the observation of one man's death but rather a spiritual disposition that draws us closer and closer to one another, deeper and deeper into the fullness of God's creation. The movement of peace present here is one of constant and determined weaving together of stories, of lives, of hopes and dreams and suffering and loss. Christ's passion reminds us that evil in the world seeks to divide, dehumanize, and pit one against another in competition. This evil, though, is named and transformed by the nonviolent Christ: Even on the cross, Jesus turns to forgive, to welcome, to include.

Is this what nonviolence invites us to? I imagine the scenes— the one on the Edmund Pettus Bridge and the one on the hilltop of Calvary—and I see these tremendous acts of courage, of vulnerability, of determination. We stare down the violence of the system at hand, one that excludes, one that insists on winners and losers, one that sees no other way besides war and a constant accumulation of wealth and resources. Our heroes of nonviolence stare all of that down, take the weight of systemic violence upon their very bodies, and expose the lies therein: No one wins an arms race; no one ever has the *most* money *forever*. Competition fractures humanity and creation, but nonviolence heals the wound, bridges the gap. We don't *need* more and more and more. We simply need one another—we need one another, each and every one of us, to flourish, to reach our potential, to discern and act on our *magis*. Solidarity is a pillar of Catholic social teaching. In some ways, it's simply empathy on a social scale. Solidarity is a principle that helps us crystallize here what the Passion requires of us, the disposition we are invited to cultivate. Much ink has been spilled on this topic, and so I simply wish to share three definitions from three different popes:

- In *Sollicitudo rei socialis*, John Paul II writes: "[Solidarity] is not a feeling of vague compassion or shallow distress at the misfortunes of so many people, both near and far. On the contrary, it is a firm and persevering determination to commit oneself to the common good; that is to say, to the good of all and of each individual, because we are all really responsible for all."[10]

- In *Caritas in veritate*, Benedict XVI writes: "To love someone is to desire that person's good and to take effective steps to secure it. Besides the good of the individual, there is the good that is linked to living in society: the common good. It is the good of 'all of us,' made up of individuals, families and intermediate groups who together constitute society. . . . To desire the *common good* and strive towards it *is a requirement of justice and charity*."[11]

- In *Fratelli tutti*, Francis writes: "Solidarity means much more than engaging in sporadic acts of generosity. It means thinking and acting in terms of community. It means that the lives of all are prior to the appropriation of goods by a few. It also means combating the structural causes of poverty, inequality, the lack of work, land and housing, the denial of social and labour rights. It means confronting the destructive effects of the empire of money . . . Solidarity, understood in its most profound meaning, is a way of making history, and this is what popular movements are doing."[12]

Solidarity and nonviolence go hand in hand. If we truly care about one another and believe in our heart of hearts that we are each imbued with God-given rights and the opportunity to reach our fullest potential, then we necessarily abhor violence done to anyone. The work of nonviolence then calls us to task. When folks use the tools of nonviolence to expose the violence lurking in the shadows of our social structures, we cannot stay silent. We cannot look idly on. We see the violence done to others made in the image and likeness of our God and recognize that the violence being done is being done in our name, in the name of upholding an inherently violent system. What do we do? How do we respond? What does solidarity demand?

Each papal reflection reminds us again and again that solidarity demands action; it is not passive. Solidarity thrusts us into history, into this moment, to meet the demands of the day. It is active just as nonviolence is active. And solidarity insists on community, on really *knowing* the fellow creatures with whom we share this existence.

The renowned Vietnamese Buddhist monk Thich Nhat Hanh introduced a concept called *interbeing*. I find it helpful in recognizing the interconnectedness of all creation—and it's a powerful way of approaching the idea that God is in all things. "We have talked about the many in the one, and the one containing many," Hanh writes in his classic text, *Being Peace*. "In one sheet of paper, we see everything else, the cloud, the forest, the logger. I am, therefore you are. You are, therefore I am. That is the meaning of the word 'interbeing.' We *inter-are*."[13] We're challenged to see every part of creation in every interaction: not just the broccoli on our plate, but the farmer who grew it and the rain that fell upon it, the cashier who handed it to us and the truck driver who transported it—a spiritual supply chain.

We weave together stories that inevitably bring us deeper into contact with one another, with all of creation. We give thanks. And in all of it, God delights.

The Passion of the Christ is the unitive way. How can we continue to do violence to one another once we truly see the sacredness of each step—each being—along the path?

Talking Ourselves onto the Cross

So what do we do? We can still so readily see Christ hanging on the cross in our world—just turn on the news. The trans youth bullied to suicide. The family forced to flee violence only to be thrust into human trafficking. The single father juggling multiple jobs just to put food on the table. The victims of abuse. Christ still hangs on the cross. Violence is everywhere and constant and cyclical. What's that old expression? *Hurt people hurt people.*

Call to mind an image of Christ on the cross for you, now. What headline? What graphic? What personal memory? I wonder if there isn't present in that story some act of division: fear of the unknown, a sense of *us* versus *them*, a fracturing of self, a scarcity mentality that demands we fight for resources lest others get them. Where is the division that breeds such hate and violence?

Now recall that unitive path of Christ's passion. Father English writes that "Christ's death on the cross and resurrection from the dead are the ultimate expression of the fact that we are indeed accepted. Jesus's death on the cross is the great sign of Christ's compassion, love and forgiveness."[14] These are active virtues—compassion, love, forgiveness—that continue to send us out into the world to bring God's peace. We can do that; we can walk that unitive path, knowing that we are accepted, that we are the beloved of God. Don't forget your inherent identity!

Embracing that identity, we then turn to disrupt the cycle of violence, and nonviolence is our tool. Rather than respond with a slap, we turn the other cheek. We're all hurt people, after all. We all carry wounds. Let's then make our mantra this: *Hurt people heal people.*

With that in mind, we go out into the world. "Jesus wants to send us out as missionaries of peace and nonviolence into the world of war and violence," John Dear reminds us.[15] That might mean attending peaceful protests, rising to heroic moments as Dorothy Day and John Lewis did. But there are quiet moments too. Ordinary moments. We are called to practice nonviolence in these instances just as much as in the louder, more noticeable moments.

I think about the times I raise my voice with my children. Are those not moments of violence, small and ordinary though they may seem? I think of my girls' own "nonviolence," and how quickly I see myself as an unjustified aggressor (read: buffoon): I lose my temper and all they're trying to do is be kids—pick out dresses, play with their toys, eat their dinner. But they don't do it *my* way, and so division rather than solidarity sets in, and I get snappy. Small, seemingly harmless, ordinary moments. Yet these are just as important, just as pattern setting, as any other moment. How do we rise to the occasion? How do we break the cycle?

I think, too, of how we treat ourselves. Do we use kind language toward ourselves, or do we berate our own actions and thoughts? Do we embrace our identity as beloved, or do we shrug and assume God meant someone else? I know how quick I am to judge my own actions—and how much higher a bar I then set for other people.

We put ourselves on the cross and then insist that everyone else hang there with us. We judge ourselves harshly and then insist everyone else be judged by the same standard. But that's the evil spirit, the enemy of our human nature. We sow seeds of division in our own hearts, and then we are shocked when irreparable conflicts erupt all over the world. Jesus's passion is the unitive way; division is of the enemy.

How are we being called to practice nonviolence today— toward ourselves, toward those we encounter most readily in our lives? We all want to be heroes of nonviolence, but sometimes—most times, really—we just need to keep quietly doing the work.

A Spiritual Exercise for Peace Work

Opening Prayer

Pray for the grace to recognize little opportunities to practice nonviolence in your daily life.

Prayer Text

His betrayer had arranged a sign with them, saying, "The man I shall kiss is the one; arrest him." Immediately he went over to Jesus and said, "Hail, Rabbi!" and he kissed him. Jesus answered him, "Friend, do what you have come for." Then stepping forward they laid hands on Jesus and arrested him. And behold, one of those who accompanied Jesus put his hand to his sword, drew it, and struck the high priest's servant, cutting off his ear. Then Jesus said to him, "Put your sword back into its sheath, for all who take the sword will perish by the sword. Do you think that I cannot call upon my Father and he will not provide me at this moment with more than twelve legions of angels? But then how would the scriptures be fulfilled which say that it must come to pass in this way?" At that hour Jesus said to the crowds, "Have you come out as against a robber, with swords and clubs to seize me? Day after day I sat teaching in the temple area, yet you did not arrest me. But all this

has come to pass that the writings of the prophets may be fulfilled."
Then all the disciples left him and fled.

Matthew 26:48–56

Reflection Exercises

- Even until the end, Jesus uses the word "friend." He wishes to invite, to include, to gather up. He wishes to heal, and he does so as a blatant act of resistance against our tendencies to violence. When you put yourself in the scene, are you a "friend" of Jesus? Do you quickly reach for your weapon? Do you desire to heal, unite, make whole?
- Ignatius has reminded us already how the evil spirit desires to work in shadow and secrecy; the Good Spirit works in the light. We see this at play in this Scripture scene—Jesus criticizes his attackers for coming to seize him under cover of night when he's spent his days preaching in the open. How are you invited to practice nonviolence to yourself and others, and how might this reminder to do so openly help you in that work?

Conversation

- In conversation with God or with neighbor, discuss what the prospect of nonviolence stirs in you—what fears, questions, hopes, or worries?
- Return to the popes' statements on solidarity. Which one strikes you most? Why?

Journal

- Who is a hero of nonviolence for you? Write out the qualities that you find most inspiring. Reflect on how those qualities are reflected in your own life.

CHAPTER 10

Risen and Returned

One of my girls received a book on Mahatma Gandhi as part of a holiday book swap at her school. It's a Little People, Big Dreams kid's book, which promptly vanished into the girls' burgeoning bookshelf. Weeks passed before I even knew we had it in the house.

"What's this?" I asked. The book lay in the middle of the girls' room, seemingly having materialized out of nowhere. "When did we get a book on Gandhi?"

"Dad!" two exasperated, little voices cried. "The book exchange at school!" Turns out I was the dumbest guy in the world. That night we settled in to read about this hero of nonviolence. Here was a person my daughters knew nothing about. To be honest, I was surprised by how little I knew.

One page describes Gandhi's expulsion from a train in South Africa: "One day, he was thrown out of a train for refusing to leave first class—a carriage that was reserved for White people only."[1] We paused there, my wife turning to the girls to draw the connection between Gandhi's experience and that of civil rights leaders such as Rosa Parks. "That's not very nice, huh?"

my wife said. The girls agreed. "It's not fair that anyone would be treated that way because of the color of their skin, right?" The girls agreed again.

The book goes on, detailing Gandhi's nonviolent resistance in South Africa and his eventual return to India to stand up to the British Empire in solidarity with the Indian people. A whole page is dedicated to his relinquishing of "his expensive British suit" in favor of "traditional Indian clothes."[2] It made Gandhi easy for my girls to spot on the remaining pages of the book. More than that, it represented an essential part of the peacebuilding puzzle: the return.

Mythologist Joseph Campbell notes in *The Hero with a Thousand Faces* that "the standard path of the mythological adventure of the hero is a magnification of the formula represented in the rites of passage: *separation—initiation—return.*" A hero necessarily leaves their status quo world in search of an adventure. In a work of fiction, that's the whole plot. Campbell says that "the hero comes back from this mysterious adventure with the power to bestow boons on his fellow man."[3] The return is essential to the story.

Gandhi, of course, is a historical figure, not a mythical one. But he is a hero to many all the same. As I read through that children's book, it struck me that his return was essential to his vocation as a man of peace. What he learned from his adventures abroad about nonviolence and peace, about injustice and hate, he brought back to his community—the would-be "boons" that were his to bestow.

Most importantly—and because Gandhi was a real person—the story continued. The cause of peace in the real world cannot be contained or solved by a word count or a run time. The story continues to unfold; it keeps going so long as there are people to live it. Thus, the return is one not solely of *endings* but of *rebirth*. The seeds of peace are planted and nurtured and grown in the community to which the hero returns.

In this chapter, we turn to the resurrection—that key moment in Jesus's story when he returns to his community. And what a "boon" he has to bestow! The Fourth Week of the Ignatian Exercises is an invitation to reflect on the resurrection. We will do exactly that here. What does it mean for us and our spirituality of peace that Ignatius ends his Exercises with the resurrection? What can we learn from this pivotal moment in the Christian story?

I'm struck again by the scene in that children's book where Gandhi gives up his expensive clothes. In many ways, he was dying to an old way of life. A dying, too, to the ways of the world—to upward mobility that insists on more money, more honors, and a bloated ego. The question here for us as we begin this chapter on resurrection and return is this: What are our "old ways" that prevent us from cultivating a posture of peace? By allowing them to die off, how will we be lighter, freer, more indifferent, and better able to then turn back to those who need us? Are these "old ways" preventing us from delving deeply into the truest needs of our community?

He's Back

The resurrection is Jesus's moment of return. During this final week of the Exercises, Ignatius invites us to pray "for the grace to be glad and rejoice intensely because of the great joy and the glory of Christ our Lord."[4] John English notes that this kind of joy "means escaping from our narrow selves to an unusual degree."[5] We accompany Christ in joy, contemplating Jesus's joy, that of those he encounters, and the joy that is consequently awakened in us. It spills over from Christ to us, from us to others, and back again. This moment of return, this turning back toward community, is key—it ignites something within us. It connects us. Saint Paul says of the body of Christ, "If one part is honored, all the parts share its joy" (1 Cor. 12:26).

Does this joy feel sudden or abrupt? We just witnessed Jesus's brutal execution, where violence was visited on his body and soul. We stood there; we watched. The disciples fled, fearful that the same violence would find and finish them. That same passage from Paul *begins* by reminding us that "if [one] part suffers, all the parts suffer with it" (1 Cor. 12:26). But now— joy! From passion to resurrection.

The transition can be jarring, yet Christ encourages us to embrace this joy, not to allow ourselves to become trapped in sorrow and sadness. To remind ourselves of our intrinsic identity as the beloved of God. "There are Christians whose lives seem like Lent without Easter," Pope Francis writes in his apostolic exhortation *Evangelii gaudium*. "I realize of course that joy is not expressed the same way at all times in life. . . . Joy adapts and changes, but it always endures, even as a flicker of light born of our personal certainty that, when everything is said and done, we are infinitely loved."[6] As we approach the resurrection, as we seek to embody its spiritual insights for peace, we must commit ourselves to that slow, steady work of joy, even in seeming darkness.

We know the story of the resurrection, more or less. Ignatius, as usual, invites us to sink into the story's scenes. Ignatius asserts that the very first of Jesus's apparitions after his return was to his mother, Mary.[7] The second was to Mary Magdalene, and then he appeared to Mary the mother of James.[8] And so on: Jesus walks with his disciples on the road to Emmaus, and he shares breakfast with his friends after a night of fishing. He appears in the upper room, even though the doors are locked, and he returns again to put Thomas's doubting mind at ease.

Ignatius names Jesus in this week the "Consoler" and says, "Consider the office of consoler that Christ our Lord exercises and compare it with the way in which friends are wont to console each other."[9] In each Gospel scene, Jesus enters deeply into the sorrow of his friends, of his community. He returns to share in that hardship, to carry it, and ultimately, to show his friends that they can let it go, that they themselves can return to their lives in a new way. Hope has spilled into joy. "The divinity, which seemed to hide itself during the passion, [is] now appearing and manifesting itself so miraculously in the most holy Resurrection."[10]

I wonder, did it *have* to be this way? Did Jesus really have to make the return journey himself? Did he have to personally visit each group of friends, spending time with each? Could we not imagine a scene parallel to Jesus's baptism at the Jordan, all his friends gathered in one place and the voice from heaven declaring, "He is risen! Fear not!" Same effect, right? In this scenario, the news of the resurrection still gets out, and the angels have a busy few days spreading the word—after all, isn't that what they did at the Incarnation?

But that's not the story we know; that's not what happened. Jesus returns. He has to come back to his friends, his beloved community. He has to console. "This is a beautiful way of showing how Jesus goes about bringing joy, hope and confidence to people," John English writes. "All of the Resurrection appearances in the Bible have the Immanuel theme—the continuation of the Incarnation today. God continues with us and is present to us."[11]

God doesn't gloss over the struggle, the fear, the hopelessness. God isn't content to give a sign in the sky as he had done at previous times. God wants to enter deeply into our own stories, to continue to walk with us from fear to hope, from uncertainty to courage, from violence to peace. "In the Resurrection appearances we hear Christ's command: 'Do not be afraid; go and tell my [friends],'" English writes. "The message of the Resurrection is 'go and spread the good news.' In other words, move out of yourself; go and tell other people."[12] There is movement in the resurrection; it is not a state of paralysis, and it is certainly not a new status quo. It is a constant calling forth.

The resurrection is an invitation to seek out and eradicate fear—the fear that closes us in on ourselves, closes us off to other people and creation, to new ways of being and thinking. The resurrection changed the story; God lifted our horizons on what was even possible. But God didn't just tell us the news; Jesus entered deeply into the story to walk with us into this new way of living.

I once heard a Jesuit preach on the ascension. He reminded us that this image of Christ going up into heaven is rather incomplete. Christ, he said, also descends into all of creation; Christ is intimately present to us now. We are the body of Christ. We are Christ's hands, Christ's feet, and so on. Rather than being solely limited to his bodily form, he can be incarnate in all things. "It is through and within the organic unity of the total Christ . . . that God's will and his creative action finally come through to us," writes Pierre Teilhard de Chardin. "Everywhere he draws us to him and brings us closer to himself, in a universal movement of convergence of spirit."[13] The resurrection and ascension become extreme acts of return, of entering ever more deeply into our spiritual home, our own selves. As Jesus shows us, the goal isn't about escaping a world riddled with violence and suffering; it's about returning to it, entering more deeply into it, and collaborating in the imaging of something more.

What does that mean for peace, then, for us to enter into the heart of things in our own community? What does it mean to turn back and return even in the wake of violence and challenge? What does it mean to recognize that *all of it* is in some way glistening with the light of the risen Christ?

Most importantly, what does it mean that we, who are made in the image and likeness of this same God who returns, are called to enter into the highs and lows of our community? How can this disposition be one of peace?

Communal Spirituality

We are also made in the image and likeness of a God who is community—three persons in one divinity. God returns to Godself; the nature of that return only highlights its necessity. So, too, with us: We are made for one another, for community. We don't simply return to our community out of the goodness of our hearts; we do so because we need to in order to understand who we fully are, to find our most authentic selves. To live out our *magis*.

It's a necessary part of our story, and it's inherent to any true peace. Conflict can be and often *is* inflicted at the behest and for the benefit of the one—a single person or entity. It only takes one person, one act of violence to cause a war. Peace, on the other hand, can be built, maintained, and made to flourish only through the work of the *many*, many threads woven together. Any peace that Jesus hoped to build required that postresurrection return. We were made to see a God who desires to labor with us in the work of peace; it is not a peace by decree, commanded at a distance.

John English provides us with helpful insights into this spiritual path. "Spirituality describes the way that we approach life in terms of our relationship to God," he writes. "It includes our sense of identity (who we are), vocation (how we are to be and what we are to do), mission (what we are to accomplish), and celebration (how we relate to others and to the earth)."[14]

That word *celebration* is an important one. It points us back to the grace for which we pray during that final week of the Exercises—that of a shared joy in Christ's resurrection. More than that, it points to how we are to conclude the Exercises, the disposition with which we should step from the Exercises and into the world.

The final meditation in Ignatius's Exercises is called the Contemplation to Attain the Love of God. My longtime spiritual director and friend, Father Jim Bowler, said to me when we reached this point in our own retreat, "I want you to write *celebrate* at the top of that page—and underline it." I did so then and am looking at that sloppy bit of handwriting now. Celebration is essential.

Here's what we're celebrating: This meditation invites us to imagine ourselves standing before God, in the company of all of God's people, basking in the many graces we have been graciously given. We are to envision ourselves living out God's dream for creation. To do that, Ignatius gives us two simple notes: "Love ought to manifest itself in deeds rather than in words"[15] and "Love consists in a mutual sharing of goods . . . the beloved shares with the lover."[16]

In short, the Contemplation to Attain Divine Love, as it is also known, is a continuation of this invitation to imagine that which seems utterly impossible: God's own dream in which peace, justice, mercy, and love reign. Ignatius gives us the recipe to begin living that way now: Allow love to be manifest through our every action. Or, remember to return again and again to the people in need, the people right here and now who need a word of peace, an act of compassion. Our community; God's people. Allow these same people to return to *us*. The love must be reciprocal.

Father English makes another important observation about spirituality. "Fundamentally, spirituality is related to our personhood," he says. "A *person* is a being in relationship with other persons, which necessarily includes a personal way of relation to the environment. This means that there is no person who is in total isolation."[17] We must love one another to most fully realize who we are as individuals. We must relate to each other if we are to be anything at all.

Peace demands community. It demands relationships—a *reordering* of relationships. Conflict, on the other hand, destroys relationships, insists we hate and distrust and do harm to one another. Conflict destroys not just the person on whom we've set our sights; conflict destroy our very selves. Peace builds us up and, in the process, all creation.

Father English provides a helpful image: "We might imagine individuals in the center of a sphere full of God's relationships with humanity. Individual spirituality focuses on the person in the center of the sphere. Communal spirituality focuses on all the relationships within the sphere. To be authentic, each spirituality needs to keep the center interacting with the rest of the sphere."[18] That, I think, is an image of peace, of love manifesting as action for the good of others.

Made in the Image of a God Who Accompanies

The earliest Jesuits recognized this challenge from the Spiritual Exercises to go out and into the world. One of the first Jesuits and a very close companion of Saint Ignatius, Jerome Nadal, captured this notion in his simple summation of Jesuit life: "We are not monks. . . . The world is our house."[19]

The Jesuits at their founding represented an entirely new way of being a religious order. At that time, to be a member of a religious community meant entering a monastery and never leaving. The idea that one could be part of a religious order *and also* be present to the needs of the world in an intimate, immediate way was novel. It took some convincing. Nadal was the man responsible for doing that work.

"If flight from the dangers of the world was the reason so many joined the Society [of Jesus]," writes the eminent Jesuit historian John O'Malley in his essential text, *The First Jesuits*, "[Nadal] needed to disabuse them of the mistaken notions about the character of the Society that this motivation seemed to imply. . . . For Nadal, in fact, the essence of the monk was 'to flee the company of other human beings.' But the essence of the Jesuit was to *seek* their company 'in order to help them.'"[20]

Part of what it meant for Jesuits to "help" was the work of peace. O'Malley writes that Nadal once "pronounced that the Jesuits were fundamentally engaged in a 'ministry of reconciliation,'" noting this is "important for understanding the other ministries and their strongly social character."[21] This work of reconciliation, which has roots in the earliest days of the Society of Jesus, continues today: "The mission of the Jesuits is a mission of justice and reconciliation, working so that women and men can be reconciled with God, with themselves, with each other and with God's creation."[22]

"That's all well and good for Jesuits," you may be thinking. "But I am not a Jesuit, so what does it matter to *me*?"

Fair question. I'm not a Jesuit either, though I work with them personally and professionally and am inspired by Ignatian spirituality. And that's more than enough—the legacy of Saint Ignatius and the spirituality that bears his name is for all people.

Even in its earliest days, the Jesuit approach demanded a deeper movement into God's creation. Again, we pursue community; we seek out the needs of others. We love and serve in all things. This activity is the work of peace. This spirituality is one that is proactive. We go to the needs; we are constantly engaging in deepening relationships. We are aware and available to act. We participate in this dance of life, weaving threads that bind us to one another. Peace demands this kind of proaction. Waiting around for conflict to start before acting allows the seeds of inaction and isolation to take root and grow into boredom, disdain, distrust, and ultimately violence.

What more might we say about this spiritual disposition? Renowned spiritual writer Margaret Silf encourages us to think of ourselves as spiritual companions. We accompany one another in a very intentional way—not unlike the risen Christ, who appears as "consoler" after the resurrection. "Spiritual companionship," Silf writes, "takes 'listening' a stage further, and reflects the ancient Celtic ministry of 'soul friendship.'

A soul friend is one who walks alongside, accompanying the spiritual journey, listening with loving attention, without judgment."[23] Do you think of yourself as someone's "soul friend"? Can you name your own such friend? This is the kind of deep engagement with one another that breeds peace.

We are all called to spiritually companion one another in this way, but as Silf makes clear, there are those *professionally* called to this sort of work. There is training that goes into it. "The essence of such training is to encourage active listening skills and to impress upon would-be companions the importance of not getting in the way in the relationship between God and the pilgrim. They are taught to listen closely and sensitively to anything the pilgrim freely chooses to share, and to reflect back to the pilgrim any aspects of the conversation that seem to be especially loaded or significant."[24]

This is important—certainly to the trainee, but also to each of us. Again, we see the wisdom from the Exercises. Silf is pointing us to the fifteenth annotation, one of twenty introductory notes Ignatius offers the director of the Exercises. The fifteenth annotation says, "Permit the Creator to deal directly with the creature, and the creature directly with [their] Creator and Lord."[25] In short, don't get in the way of God and God's beloved. Why? This is the essential insight: *Because God is still unfolding in each of us.* We know that we were made in the image and likeness of God, but we too often forget that God is still working within us. The fifteenth annotation is the reminder we need—when dealing with others, but also when looking at ourselves.

God is still at work here, now, in me, in you. What possibilities, then, await us as we return to our community, as we accompany one another—each of us carrying God dwelling within us? Does God in me seek out and desire God in you? The Good Spirit weaves those threads of peace together; the evil spirit desires nothing more than that we isolate ourselves and, subsequently, do violence to our God, who dwells within each of us.

Little Returns of Peace

I return to that opening anecdote and the story of Gandhi. His return to his people was truly one of peace, an act of bravery and determination that changed the world. I don't know how often, if ever, I'll get such a chance in my own life story. But I can still look to Gandhi—to this inherent trajectory of a peace-that-returns—and be inspired in my own life. While I may not be traveling from one country to another to inspire a movement for justice, I certainly make my own returns—to my family, to my colleagues, to my cats. What disposition do I bring with me? How can it be one of peace?

I think about when I return from a trip, how I'm refilled and refreshed and that much more patient with my kids. I have new stories to share and questions to ask when I return to the office. What have I missed? What have others been up to? The return should make me curious about others, about their stories, and that curiosity can become a bridge to another.

We make little returns all the time: to that store at the mall, to our friend's house, to the bus stop. Each time is a new opportunity to be curious, to look anew at a well-known place with wonder and awe, to show grace to the people we meet there. That circular path is a natural one in our human story, a natural rhythm, a natural opportunity to be thrust into the mix again and again. Each time, we have the chance to strengthen a relationship: a smile at the cashier, a kindness in the parking lot, a charitable interpretation of a fellow driver's abrasiveness. These are little seeds of peace that we can water each time we make our return. Seeds that blossom into joy through our little acts of love.

Today, you'll have such a chance. Don't miss it.

A Spiritual Exercise for Peace Work

Opening Prayer

Pray for the grace to make a return of peace to any individual, any aspect of creation that you see anew this day.

Prayer Text

Now that very day two of them were going to a village seven miles from Jerusalem called Emmaus, and they were conversing about all the things that had occurred. And it happened that while they were conversing and debating, Jesus himself drew near and walked with them, but their eyes were prevented from recognizing him. He asked them, "What are you discussing as you walk along?" They stopped, looking downcast. One of them, named Cleopas, said to him in reply, "Are you the only visitor to Jerusalem who does not know of the things that have taken place there in these days?" And he replied to them, "What sort of things?" They said to him, "The things that happened to Jesus the Nazarene. . . . Some women from our group, however, have astounded us: they were at the tomb early in the morning and did not find his body; they came back and reported that they had indeed seen a vision of angels who announced that he was alive. Then some of those with us went to the tomb and found things just as the women had described, but him they did not see." . . . Then beginning with Moses and all the prophets, [Jesus] interpreted to them what referred to him in all the scriptures. . . . Then they said to each other, "Were not our hearts burning [within us] while he spoke to us on the way and opened the scriptures to us?" So they set out at once and returned to Jerusalem.

Luke 24:13–19, 22–24, 27, 32–33

Reflection Exercises

- This Scripture passage gives us a clear sense of *walking away*. We see two disciples actively trying not to return. But Jesus won't have it. He accompanies them, even going so far as to walk alongside them as they go in the *wrong* direction. But that's part of accompaniment, part of Jesus's mission. What is the importance of Christ's convincing these two to return to Jerusalem? Is Christ inviting you to make a return?

- Jesus approaches his friends with curiosity. How does a disposition of curiosity make us more available for the work of peace?

Conversation

- In conversation with God or with neighbor, reflect on the many returns in your own life. When have you embodied peace? When have you struggled to do so?

Journal

- The Jesuits have not always lived up to the ideals embedded in their spiritual tradition, but because the world itself is their monastery, they are, at their best, curious about God's continued, unfolding work in creation. Their spirituality is one that develops. How has your own spirituality unfolded in new ways? How does your own learning contribute to your own desire for peace?

CHAPTER 11

The Spirit of Creativity Brings Peace

Our girls make a lot of art. I mean, *a lot* of art. And it's not all—how do I say this delicately?—*good*. Like, is that scribble of yellow crayon on an otherwise completely white scrap of paper "art"? I wouldn't put it in a museum, personally. But . . .

"Daddy, I made this for you!"

"Oh . . . thanks. It's . . . beautiful. I . . . love it." You can really feel those pauses, right?

"I'll put it in your office!" Scamper, scamper go little feet, and the pile of quasi-colorful pieces of paper in my office gets that much higher.

Now listen, I'm not the worst parent. My girls make cool stuff sometimes—creative, complex, beautiful. Sometimes they bring these pieces of art home from school, other times they make art magic right there in our sunroom. These we keep; these we put on the fridge. But those pieces that barely have anything resembling drawing on them at all, those quick, slapdash,

"the crayon barely touched the paper" masterpieces? I mean
. . . What am I supposed to do with those?

My wife and I—again, not terrible parents—have had a
few conversations about this. To be honest, that pile of art in
my office is much too high and only contributes to an already
chaotic desk. My wife, too, can't keep hanging things on her
bookshelf—there's just not that much shelf. But what do we do?

"We can't tell them to stop," I say, half-hoping my wife will
disagree.

"No, of course not," she says in reply.

"Maybe we tell them just to keep the good stuff?"

"But they get so sad when we recycle what they've made . . . "

"Exactly," I say. "I have an idea."

That weekend, I bought each girl a three-ring binder. "This
is where you put your *special* art—the stuff you're really proud
of," I told them, thinking that the very process of selection
would solve the problem for us. The girls were excited; twenty
minutes of enthusiastic three-ring hole punching ensued.
Then the binders were full and forgotten—and the art kept
coming.

Let's stop here for a moment. I want you to check your own
feelings about this story. How would you respond? How *have*
you responded? I bet that while you agree we can't just keep
hanging or piling up pieces of scrap paper all over the house,
you also instinctively agree that we can't tell our children to
stop being creative. To stop imagining. To stop making new
things. To stop finding space to create.

And why? Because creativity, forming an imagination, and
dreaming are beautiful, important, life-giving skills. Virtues,
even. I desperately want my little girls to be creative, imaginative, beautiful people.

Here's another thing: My girls' art is improving. We still get
the occasional yellow scribble, but each time they put crayon
or paintbrush or the forbidden Sharpie marker to paper, their

art gets better. More complex. More beautiful. Their creativity bears more and more fruit.

It's not hard to see the growth in their art. The point is not for them to submit their pieces to contests or enter art school—though certainly if they'd like to one day, I'll be more than supportive. The point is that through that dogged, creative determination, they express themselves with deeper, more poignant clarity. They discover new things about their own artistic selves, and they grow in excitement over what they're able to make.

Ignatian spirituality does not have a monopoly on creativity, but the Ignatian tradition *does* have a rich history of and tools for cultivating a creative spirit, of marrying spirituality and our artistic selves together. And creativity, I believe, is essential to any peace work. Creativity is essential to any vocation. How else do we dream up or imagine the kind of person we might yet become? In this chapter, we return once more to creativity as an avenue for bringing about peace, both within ourselves and within our world.

The Ignatian Imagination Revisited

Let's revisit that all-important cannonball moment. Ignatius gets knocked down. The life he'd expected to lead dissipates before him. Where does he go next? Back to the castle, back to Loyola, back to bed. The man has to recover—and it's not a quick process.

In the daydreaming that ensues, Ignatius sees two paths forward: one, a return to courtly life, albeit with a limp and chip on his shoulder. That old way of living—the wars and the women—leaves him feeling empty. The Spirit presents him with a second option: *What if you strive for holiness? What if you become a pilgrim, an ambassador for God and God's people?*

This period of daydreaming gets plenty of airtime in the telling and retelling of Ignatius's story. It's important, of course—God speaks to Ignatius through his dreams, through his imagination. And Ignatius listens; he responds to the Spirit's prompting. From there, he goes on to encounter God more deeply, to pen the Spiritual Exercises and to help found the Society of Jesus.

But let's focus on this period of daydreaming, of imagining. I believe we have here an essential invitation for peace, a building block that is too easily dismissed or rushed through. What are the cannonball strikes in your life? They come in many forms: a loved one's sickness, anxiety over a new job, a rocky relationship, the highs and lows of parenting, or the unique challenge we each face to find purpose and meaning. These are personal strains on our inner peace.

What about at the societal level? Within our communities, what cannonball strikes destroy our peace? Environmental injustice, gun violence, loneliness and addiction, families forced to flee their homes. We may see these things at a theoretical level, but once they hit us—once we are directly affected by any of these societal struggles—it feels different. Our lives torn asunder, we find ourselves thrown off balance. Peace dissipates as quickly as Ignatius's life goals. And what happens next?

There is an invitation here, and I would like to offer it to you—and to seize on it myself. In these moments of unpeace, when our personal lives are rocked and our communities are shaken, I invite each of us to pause, to step back. To recognize the cannonball strike for what it is and to then take a moment to dream up what comes next. We are so accustomed to go-go-going, to responding to chaos and hardship in stride, that the very idea of pausing, as Ignatius was forced to do, to take account of the violence done to our sense of self and our community might seem, at best, impractical.

Very few of us can take eleven months off, as Ignatius did—much to his chagrin, I might add. Many of us may be unable to take even a day or two to recover from our own cannonball strikes. I understand this; I understand that many of us are indeed caught up in the grind of life. This is unfair and unfortunate. So, I simply invite you to take what you can, to pause—if even for an hour or two—and allow yourself to grieve, to think, to pray, to ponder. Don't make excuses for yourself; don't allow shame and guilt to sneak in and rob you of this momentary reprieve. This time is yours—and it is necessary to find the peace God desires to give.

A moment of peace is important, but the Ignatian tradition shows us something else too. We don't just daydream for the sake of daydreaming; we daydream so as to dream ourselves into a new way of being. Ignatius didn't just read about the saints; he didn't just dream about the saints. He imagined himself *becoming* one. He tried that new way of life on for size. The impact of his dreaming went well beyond his own personal fulfillment—it changed the world.

I wonder: Can we unravel the big injustices of our time, the greatest sources of conflict and suffering, if we don't first imagine a better way forward? Can we solve the climate crisis already at hand if we don't pause to dream up the kind of world we desire to save, the kind of world we want to live in? In this dreaming, do we then discover a unique role for ourselves? Do we see where God calls us—you and me—to *act* in response to what we *see*?

The purpose of the Spiritual Exercises of Saint Ignatius of Loyola is to discern God's will—God's greatest dream and desire—for our lives and to act on it. We know God loves us, that God desires happiness and flourishing for each of us. We know God wants each of us to act on our own unique *magis*— and in so doing, discover the peace God wishes for us.

That's at the microlevel. But the same is true at the macrolevel. God does not will violence or evil, so how do we get back to God's original dream of peace? Return again to where the Exercises began, where we looked clearly and honestly at the chaos of the world, where we considered where we are versus where God wants us to be. We must allow ourselves to be moved—to be knocked off our feet—by the overwhelming sense of hurt and injustice that so often grips our hearts and our world.

The late Catholic priest and Missionary of the Precious Blood Robert J. Schreiter, notes that the story of God's covenant with Noah shows us God's desire to remind humanity of the original architecture of peace laid out in creation: "In this covenant God reveals the nature of the world order—how human beings are to live with one another, with the animals and with the earth."[1] For Schreiter, there was an original design for peace, for the working of all creation. But things go badly, and God has to pivot. The peace first understood in the nature of creation itself needs further clarifying; the natural way of things is not playing out as it should—just look around you!

According to Schreiter, then, there is a phase two. "If the first peace, based on creation, is peace revealed to all humankind, then this peace is a peace redeemed, one that results from an acknowledgment of the incapacity of human beings to extricate themselves entirely from the mess they have made of God's creations, and God's intervention to make of us a new creation."[2]

I'm struck by this notion that something has stalled in the natural working of things. That the peace God desires is not occurring as it should. That our own imaginations are so limited, so stifled by violence, that it's hard for us to even see a way out. (This might remind us of the structural and cultural violence of previous chapters.)

So what must we do? Schreiter says this: "That God gives the gift of peace to those who strive to live in right relationship underscores the fact that God is with creation at all times and is not a distant God."[3] In the Ignatian tradition, we know God to be very near indeed—in all things, in fact—and certainly

172

present in our imagination, our desires, and our hopes. We know that God desires to work *with* us, to have us as collaborators in building up a world of justice and peace; we are, after all, called to *love* and *serve* within the world. As the fifteenth annotation insists, the Creator desires to deal directly with us, the beloved creatures, as we strive to understand and live out our vocations.

I believe if we are to respond to that invitation to love and serve, if we are to come closer to realizing God's dream of peace for ourselves and for our world, we must assume a more creative, playful, spontaneous disposition. John Paul Lederach invites us to consider *art* as a way to peace, saying, "The artistic process initially breaks beyond what can be rationally understood and then returns to a place of understanding that may analyze, think it through, and attach meaning to it."[4] When we face the overwhelming nature of suffering and violence, an artistic spirit can keep us from falling back into the old ways of doing things. Don't jump right to the rational; dwell first in the creative. The old ways have failed us; we must dream up new ones.

Lederach continues: "This is much like the process of reconciliation. Brokenness wanders all over our souls. Healing requires a similar journey of wandering."[5] We know what it is to be broken—we've been hit by that cannonball, after all. But do we allow ourselves to *wander*? Put yourself back into that moment in Ignatius's story, his own mental wanderings while healing in bed and his eventual worldly wanderings— a pilgrimage of body and soul. In these wanderings, God speaks. The Spirit acts on our lives in surprising ways, but if we are rigid, if we insist on repeating old mistakes, on doing things the way they've always been done, we fail in our quest for peace.

So let us explore what a spirituality of creativity might require.

Cultivating the Artist Spirit

I'm always struck by the number of Jesuit artists who have left their mark on the world. Many know the famous English Jesuit and poet Gerard Manley Hopkins, who, during his relatively short life in the 1800s, reminded us that "the world is charged with the grandeur of God."[6] But Hopkins is not alone. There are Jesuit poets and playwrights, novelists and screenwriters. There are Jesuits who dance and Jesuits who make music.

What's more, Jesuit life has often been examined through the lens of art. I remember watching *The Mission* in high school more times than I can count, the tragic tale of Jesuit missionaries and the community they served in South America. Mary Doria Russell's classic novel *The Sparrow* and its sequel, *Children of God*, take themes of Jesuit missionary life out into space among literal alien races. And if you push further, Jesuits have been heroes and villains in stories told around the world.

I'm not suggesting we all run out and write Jesuit-inspired poems. I'm suggesting instead that we turn to curiosity, to wonder, to a desire to mine the depths of this spiritual tradition that seems so ripe for creative harvest. Let's turn again to Lederach, who so succinctly connects the artist and the peacebuilder:

> The goal of bridging art and peacebuilding is not that we endeavor to become something we are not. Nor is it the pursuit of the "arts" in order to find a way to somehow become miraculously gifted in one of the forms, like music, poetry, or painting. Experimenting and working at those can create tremendous insight, inner strength and sustenance. But I am not appealing for nor advocating that peacebuilders must be artists in the professional sense of the word in order to connect art and social change. The key is simpler than that: We must find a way to touch the sense of art the lies within us all.[7]

Chris Pramuk, the Chair of Ignatian Thought and Imagination at Regis University, wrote a beautiful book called *The Artist Alive: Explorations in Music, Art, and Theology*. In it, he invites us to cultivate our own inner artist spirit, to find that sense of wonder and curiosity already beating within us. We must touch this part of our vocation, the part that opens us up to new and creative horizons. But this takes sustained effort. It's a discipline, a practice. He says that "the capacity for wonder is not enough. If we do not cultivate the will to wonder in ourselves, our children . . . it risks atrophying and dying in us a slow but inevitable death."[8] This would be tragic because it's this will to wonder that bridges our creative selves with our hope for peace. "The will to wonder is a subversive act, an act of resistance against every force of distraction or despair that would deaden our attunement to life's possibilities."[9]

The artist spirit alive within us—our own unique creative spirituality—is a powerful thing. It grants us the ability to make space, to hold within ourselves a sacred chamber within which we can dream up that which is not yet possible. From there, our inner space spills out and over into the very real world, and we invite others to engage their own creative selves. "To the artist and poet, the mystic and prophet, such awareness is the beginning of insight, the seed bud of unforeseen possibilities springing to life in the pregnant spaces between freedom and imagination," Pramuk writes.[10] For our dream of peace, creativity means we imagine a new way of telling the story, a new role for our characters. Cannonball moments rightly shift our identities and those of the people around us. Can we come back to ourselves post-cannonball strike renewed and refreshed and ready to dream bigger about who we are and who we might yet be in community?

Ultimately, we need to continue working at imagining a God who is big enough, inclusive enough, loving enough for all of us. Because in truth, that is the nature of God; we've just not expanded our imaginations enough to grapple with that reality. Ignatian spirituality gives us spiritual tools with which to enter into this work, with which to energize our imaginations. We make that necessary space in our lives and in our schedules to allow the Spirit to speak, to create with the raw material of our dreams. Then we enter into those dreams in a bodily, fully incarnated way. As Ignatius suggests, we engage our senses, we contemplate the real and allow it to inform our imagination. Then we turn back to that God of surprises who takes both the *real* and the *imagined* and ushers us into a world that needs us to love both.

That's where we are called to practice hope—hope in what might yet be, hope in who we might yet be for one another. We pray for the grace to desire that which God desires, even if we cannot yet fully see it.

Our God of Surprises

As an undergraduate student I took a course called Writing and Responding. The professor who taught the course, Betsy Bowen, also oversaw the writing center, so students who passed her class could then apply to be tutors at the center. Thus, many of Bowen's assignments were given with an eye to the possibility that we might soon accompany other young writers finding and fine-tuning their voices.

One assignment in her class has stuck with me. The task was to reflect on an aspect of writing that had another, nonwriting meaning. A computer, for example, can be a writing tool. It can also be a purveyor of cat videos, a means with which to communicate with loved ones on the other side of the world, and an item you wouldn't want to forget at a hotel. The assignment was to write about the computer as a writing tool through the lens of one of these other ways of understanding the device. As far as assignments go, this one was peculiar, confusing, and spectacular.

For my assignment, I was fascinated by the blank space of a fresh piece of paper or a blank screen. Think of the potential! The possibility! But also the fear, the anxiety, the unknown. That's what blank space can be, right? Full of all those things and more.

Naturally, because I am who I am—a guy who has also written an entire book on Ignatian spirituality and *Star Wars*[11]—I could not get out of my head the classic mantra from *Star Trek*: "Space: the final frontier." What if I wrote about a blank piece of paper through the lens of this beloved sci-fi refrain?

Not to brag, but I do recall doing quite well on that paper. Dr. Bowen was pleased, and I joined the writing center staff the following year. But that project was more than just a goofy way to use my love of speculative storytelling to pass a class; it unwittingly set the tone for how I think about writing even to this day.

What do our intrepid crews of various starships across the *Star Trek* franchise do? They boldly go where no one has gone before. They journey into the unknown of space with all their fear and excitement and anxiety and hope, and they chart new paths. They make new friends and discover new lands, and they imagine a new way of being—and, importantly, of being *together*.

That's what the blank page of a writing project can mean. That's what the blank space of any creative project *is* at its outset. We hold that space as sacred, as brimming with possibility, and then we make our mark. We muddle through and erase words and circle back and realize we've lost the plot. We employ our erasers and call for an editor and do it all over again. If we're doing it right, we find ourselves perhaps more than a bit surprised at the project's conclusion. We might call that the Spirit at work. And the Spirit works in similarly nonlinear, surprising ways in our efforts for peace.

I rarely sit down to write without a rather clear idea of where I plan to go. Regardless, nearly every time, the direction changes, the trajectory is adjusted—if I am open to it, if I am attentive to what's happening on the page and in my own being. Even the manuscript for this book has taken shape in ways I did not anticipate when I was outlining the project. And I think that's good. I think that's right. I think that's how creativity works and how the artist spirit alive in each of us manifests itself.

I think that's God. For me, a writer, writing is a form of prayer, of understanding the world and my role within it. That's how creativity informs our vocation; it's yeast that demands our soul rise higher and with joy.

Is this a groundbreaking solution to the violence that ails so much of our world? Perhaps not, but it is a disposition. It is a practice. It is a way in which we can hold ourselves in this troubled land. We make that space within ourselves, within our lives, within the lives of others, and we bless it as sacred, because we know in that space, our God of surprises is at work. That "space" in your life may be a room in which friends or strangers gather; it may be a journal with blank pages. It may be a moment of peace and quiet before we start our days; it may be little more than a mug, empty before filled with coffee.

Let God work in that space. Let God surprise you. Let God invite you to God's holy work. And hear yourself respond— your voice echoing in that empty space that will soon be full of God's Spirit.

This is ultimately why my wife and I choose to keep hanging our daughters' artwork on the wall. Sure, give me another piece of paper with three green squiggles and a sticker. Because you know what? That space is sacred—and they acted within it. They found that holy ground and did something new, something that came from within themselves. As Pramuk reminds us, this capacity to wonder must be nurtured, must be formed, must be cultivated.

The cannonball strike forced Ignatius to stumble into his own sacred space of daydreaming and prayer. But whether he realized it in the moment, whether he intended it or not, that space proved essential. It allowed him to dream up something new. He could have dismissed it. He could have expressed irritation at so many months of boredom; instead, Ignatius found God in that space—a space inherited through hardship and suffering, but sacred just the same.

In these holy spaces of contemplation and wonder and awe, we discover something new within ourselves, something new within our world. Emboldened by this mysterious bit of hope, we act for the common good. We create peace.

A Spiritual Exercise for Peace Work

Opening Prayer

Pray for the grace to be surprised and inspired by the Spirit of Creativity alive and active in your life.

Prayer Text

And suddenly there came from the sky a noise like a strong driving wind, and it filled the entire house in which they were. Then there appeared to them tongues as of fire, which parted and came to rest on each one of them. And they were all filled with the holy Spirit and began to speak in different tongues, as the Spirit enabled them to proclaim. . . .

Then Peter . . . proclaimed to them, ". . . These people are not drunk, as you suppose, for it is only nine o'clock in the morning. No, this is what was spoken through the prophet Joel:

'It will come to pass in the last days,' God says,
'that I will pour out a portion of my spirit
upon all flesh.
Your sons and your daughters shall prophesy,
your young men shall see visions,
your old men shall dream dreams.
Indeed, upon my servants and my handmaids
I will pour out a portion of my spirit in those days,
and they shall prophesy.'"

Acts 2:2–4, 14–18

Reflection Exercises

- In the Scripture passage, the working of the Holy Spirit con-fuses those who witness it. But the disciples act boldly all the same in proclaiming a new way of living. How does this mirror the Spirit of Creativity alive now in you and your community? How can your own holy boldness usher in peace?

- Peter reminds us that the Spirit brings many gifts and bears many fruits in our lives. What might you pray for particularly in your own desire for peace?

Conversation

- In conversation with God or with neighbor, discuss what it means for *you* to be creative. How would you define it? Do you naturally consider yourself a creative person? Or do you bristle at the notion? Why?

- How might you make time for the artist spirit alive in you to grow and flourish? How has that artist spirit helped you re-spond to cannonball moments in your life and in others?

Journal

- Write down all the ways you have been creative in the last week. Reflect on how God might be using this creativity, however defined, to bring about peace and love in our world.

CHAPTER 12

Forgiveness

Broken and Shared

For me as a Catholic, any notion of forgiveness or reconciliation calls to mind the sacrament of penance, or more simply, confession. In the Catholic Church, there are seven sacraments, and the sacrament of penance is typically the second you receive (after baptism). Since I was so young—just in second grade—when I first received this sacrament, so much of my formative and religious thinking around these essential ideas of reconciliation, forgiveness, and confession have been framed by this sacramental experience. The whole purpose of this sacrament *is* reconciliation, a restoring and repairing of relationship with self, with God, and with neighbor. Confession should lead us to peace.

Generally, I've had a positive experience of confession, but I'm not the norm. I think this particular sacrament is often misunderstood and misused. The very mention of *confession* likely conjures an image of a dark, musty room and a mean old priest who's overly interested in your private affairs. (I'm sorry if that's happened to you.) "Why can't I simply confess directly to God?" you might wonder. "I don't need the priest or his poorly lit room." (I understand how you feel.)

It's not the purpose of this book to explain or justify the theological implications of the sacrament of penance, but I will say that this sacramental experience necessitates three elements I consider essential to any true experience of reconciliation and peace: a reflection on our own actions, an encounter with another person, and a clear and direct reminder that we are believed and beloved.

We've seen these three elements at work in this book and in the Ignatian tradition. The Examen—that daily Ignatian prayer—is meant to intentionally walk us through our day in the company of God's Spirit to identify both where we've realized God's dream for ourselves and others and where we might yet have opportunities to do so. Before the sacrament of penance, we are encouraged to pray through a similar examination of our lives. The sacrament itself should not be simply a litany of where we've fallen short but also a celebration of and gratitude for where God has been at work in our stories. Too many of us, though, are taught and tempted to focus solely on the negative.

Can you confess your shortcomings directly to God? Of course you can. But there's something to be said about encountering another person, about finding the voice within ourselves to say aloud those things for which we are grateful and for which we desire help. The Ignatian tradition encourages us to find spiritual companions along our pilgrimage to God; we need one another because we go to God together. In the sacrament of confession, we encounter another person who assures us that God never tires of forgiving us.

In that final point, we hear clearly, concisely (or at least, we *should*) that we are believed, forgiven, and most importantly, beloved by God. For me, there is something important about hearing those words from another person, about being reminded that God is still with me, delighting. We know this truth at a theoretical level and at a theological level. But sometimes we just need to *hear* it. We need the words to sink into the depths of our souls.

Ultimately, that sacramental experience is ritualistic. It marks a threshold in our lives. It disrupts our story. It allows us to start anew. *You are believed. You are forgiven. You are beloved.* And we begin again. We continue onward. We need not be weighed down by past failings; we need to mend those old wounds so that we can birth something new.

In this final chapter, we will meditate on this important spiritual practice of forgiveness, both for ourselves and for others. What keeps us from practicing it? What new horizons for peace might open up if we do?

Cannonball Memories

The Gospel of Mark tells us to "love your neighbor as yourself" (12:31). We often forget the *yourself* part, so understandably focused we might be on the needs of our neighbor. However, without loving ourselves we can never properly learn to love our neighbor—and loving our neighbor is essential in building a world of peace. We need to learn to forgive ourselves, lest we become paralyzed and unable to love and serve those around us.

Ignatius of Loyola's life story is a prime example of such paralysis. Return for a moment to those months he spent recovering in bed after the cannonball strike. What guilt did he feel? What shame? What remorse and sorrow? He wasn't simply remembering his courtly endeavors or his foolishness with women; he was sitting in the immediate aftermath of having unnecessarily sent so many of his fellow soldiers to their deaths.

God called Ignatius all the same. The would-be saint wasn't meant to stay stuck in his old ways or in his bed—he was meant to get up and be about God's work. Again and again, though, that guilt and shame and doubt set in. Most memorably, Ignatius was tormented in the cave outside Manresa while he penned the Spiritual Exercises. The evil spirit insisted that Ignatius could never be strong enough to live the life God invited him to, so why should he even bother?

This passage from Ignatius's autobiography (again, written in the third person) captures well the man's struggles: "[Ignatius] began to have much trouble from scruples, for even though the general confession he had made at Montserrat had been quite carefully done and all in writing . . . still at times it seemed to him that he had not confessed certain things. This caused him much distress." So, despite his own confession, he found no solace. A new tack was taken: "His confessor ordered him not to confess anything of the past unless it was something quite clear. But since he found all those things to be very clear, this order was of no use to him."[1] Ignatius couldn't shake the sense that he would never be enough. He couldn't forgive himself for his past shortcomings—even after hearing repeatedly that God had forgiven him, that God loved him.

How often do we find ourselves trapped in such a useless cycle? Again and again we turn a past mistake or failure over in our mind, unable to break free, unable to right our wrongs and move forward. If we entrap ourselves in our own sins, how much more likely are we to reduce others to *their* greatest sins? We hide our shame and instead point out the errors in another. We allow our shortcomings to eat away at our inner life and any chance of peace, and we ourselves become tormentors, agitators, unravelers of peace in the lives of our community members.

It would take Ignatius a long time to discern that this was the working of the evil spirit. That's why in the Spiritual Exercises, he commits a whole section to scruples. He writes, "If one has a delicate conscience, the evil one seeks to make it excessively sensitive, in order to disturb and upset it more easily. . . . If one has a lax conscience, the enemy endeavors to make it more so."[2] The enemy pushes upon our weaknesses, trying to expose and manipulate them. While it makes sense that a lax conscience would easily lend itself to further dissipation of just and moral action, it might not be as easy to name our own efforts at self-improvement or self-discipline as a point in which we are tempted away from what is good and right.

Failing to forgive ourselves and being paralyzed by self-doubt and recrimination become a way in which God's good work is stifled. Instead, it is better to recognize our mistakes and our weaknesses, and muddle on all the same, imperfect though we may be. We look honestly at our own failures, but then we commit to keep going forward.

Forgiveness Takes Practice

It's not easy to forgive ourselves, just as it's not easy to forgive others. We do terrible things; others do terrible things to us and to those we love. Perhaps we cannot forgive in one fell swoop. Instead, we take little steps, shuffling in the direction we hope to go. If we see in Ignatius's story—and perhaps in our own—a failure to forgive as an act resulting in paralysis, we can see forgiveness itself as a way to allow the story to continue. God's Spirit is able to work, even in these little, tiny, perhaps unnoticed acts of forgiveness. We resist paralysis; we push onward. We trust God's Spirit to work because, ultimately, we want to love our neighbors as we love ourselves. We're all in this together.

"Forgiveness and love of enemy, which are essential to genuine reconciliation, are virtues that one cannot simply draw from one's pocket at the negotiating table. They presuppose a life-long practice of outstanding generosity and humility that can hardly be expected from most people," writes Sister Mary John Mananzan, OSB. She is an activist and Missionary Benedictine nun from the Philippines who has developed an Asian feminist theology of liberation. "Christian peacemakers believe in a God who is Love and who, out of that love, took on human flesh, shared in human suffering, forgave his accusers and tormentors and empowered his followers to forgive as well. There are some transgressions that make forgiveness seem impossible; only grace makes it possible to forgive the unforgivable."[3]

I take some comfort in these words—radical forgiveness and love of enemy is *not* easy. But it is God's dream for our world; it is the foundation upon which we imagine a new way of living. And it takes constant practice, practice that begins again with *us*. "The transformation of our view of enemies has less to do with our capacity to see them differently—at least initially—than with our experience of how God heals us in the act of reconciliation and, in turn, brings us to a difference place," writes Father Robert J. Schreiter, C.PP.S.[4] Again, true peace liberates both the oppressor and the oppressed alike.

In her book *The Ignatian Guide to Forgiveness*, Marina McCoy—a professor of philosophy at Boston College—encourages us to return to that final mediation from the Spiritual Exercises, the Contemplation to Attain Divine Love. "I consider all the gifts that God has given me," she writes, reminding us of the meditation's ultimate goal. "I meditate on how God tirelessly labors for me and works on my behalf in all things. At the end, I return all these gifts to God so that God can use them in whatever way God desires."[5] The Contemplation to Attain Divine Love is an exercise in gratitude and indifference—cornerstones of Ignatian spirituality. But what if we used this meditation to practice forgiveness?

"One way to bring this process of forgiving to a close is to pray with these same kinds of ideas," McCoy writes. She offers a number of simple steps:

1. Call to mind examples of people who have done the work of forgiveness and reconciliation. Who are they? How do they inspire us?
2. Reflect: "What gifts have I received in undertaking this process of forgiveness? What have I learned? How have I been graced?"
3. Finally, make a return: "I last offer this back to God so that God can use the good of this work for peace and forgiveness in whatever ways God might want to in the future."[6] Peace built upon Ignatian indifference.

Ultimately, we want to forgive ourselves so as to allow our own *magis* to be unleashed into the world; we don't want to stifle God's dream or our part in God's story. Then, quite simply, we love our neighbor as we love ourselves. A failure to forgive sows seeds of violence, from which we will harvest nothing but division and hate and suffering. The act of forgiveness, of reconciliation, binds our wounds and brings us back together. It disrupts the cycle of endless violence and allows new possibilities to be born.

You may have noted the importance of humility in this work of forgiveness. Sister Mananzan names it outright in the line quoted earlier as a necessary practice in order to make ourselves available to act on God's dream of reconciliation. As we've seen throughout this book—and certainly in this chapter—holding tightly to our own sense of ego, our own pride and insistence on a certain status quo is an impediment to peace. Humility, too, is a clear indicator of the standard of Christ. And so, here in this final chapter on reconciliation, as we conclude our reflection on loving ourselves so as to better love our neighbor, I share with you a quote from Saint Francis de Sales that I have found to be a powerful antidote to the sort of scruples that paralyzed Ignatius—and that so often continue to wreak havoc on my own inner life.

Humility causes us to avoid troubling ourselves about our own imperfections by remembering those of others: for why should we be more perfect that others?—and in the same way to avoid troubling ourselves over those of others when we remember our own: for why should we think it extraordinary for others to have imperfections since we have plenty? Humility makes our hearts gentle towards the perfect and the imperfect; towards those from reverence, towards these from compassion.[7]

A Spiritual Exercise for Peace Work

Opening Prayer

Pray for the grace to forgive freely and to accept the forgiveness freely given.

Prayer Text

But to you who hear I say, love your enemies, do good to those who hate you, bless those who curse you, pray for those who mistreat you. To the person who strikes you on one cheek, offer the other one as well, and from the person who takes your cloak, do not withhold even your tunic. Give to everyone who asks of you, and from the one who takes what is yours do not demand it back. Do to others as you would have them do to you. For if you love those who love you, what credit is that to you? Even sinners love those who love them. And if you do good to those who do good to you, what credit is that to you? Even sinners do the same. If you lend money to those from whom you expect repayment, what credit [is] that to you? Even sinners lend to sinners, and get back the same amount. But rather, love your enemies and do good to them, and lend expecting nothing back; then your reward will be great and you will be children of the Most High, for he himself is kind to the ungrateful and the wicked. Be merciful, just as [also] your Father is merciful.

Stop judging and you will not be judged. Stop condemning and you will not be condemned. Forgive and you will be forgiven.

Luke 6:27–37

Reflection Exercises

- This can be a challenging passage. Allow yourself to linger over one or two lines that really strike you. What about them unsettles you? How might God be speaking to you through them?
- What kind of world is this passage envisioning? What steps might we take to begin to realize it in our daily lives?

Conversation

- In conversation with God or with neighbor, name those obstacles in your life to forgiveness—both of yourself and your neighbor. How might you overcome them with God's grace?
- It's easy to look at our world and name people who have committed seemingly unforgivable sins. And yet, we are still called to forgive. How might forgiveness lead us toward peace, even in these difficult instances?

Journal

- We do not need to make sweeping gestures of peace; we can simply take one small step at a time. List five to ten small steps you can take to begin building a bridge toward peace.

Conclusion

Simple Seeds of Peace

On the day the World Trade Center was attacked on September 11, 2001, and the world mourned the effects of profound evil yet again, I was in seventh grade and scheduled to have soccer practice.

"We should cancel it," I told my dad. He was one of the coaches, and I was always looking for an excuse to get out of any sort of athletic endeavor.

"No," my dad replied.

"But—what happened in New York!" I replied, shocked.

My dad then said something that has stuck with me for all these years: "That's the whole point of terrorism. They want to disrupt our daily lives. That's why we're going to have soccer practice tonight."

I didn't fully understand his point then, but I appreciate it now. My soccer practice didn't heal any of the gaping wounds opened that day. It didn't bring back the dead or help anyone process trauma and grief. It didn't prevent the wars and conflicts that quickly followed in the wake of so much anger and

193

sorrow and hate and vengeance, nor did it end the sale of arms across the globe.

But we pulled on our cleats and strapped on our shin guards and took to the field that evening all the same. While we kids knew so little of what had happened and what was about to happen, our parents and others—those who were able to be on the field that night—were able to gather together and mourn.

No matter who you were or where you lived, it was a trying, challenging day. But it was better—as my dad knew—to process that day in community. I'm struck by that image: a ragtag group of parents staggering out of their homes, kids in tow bearing soccer balls in the wake of global tragedy to take to the soccer field for an hour or so of meaningless and all-important, normalcy-maintaining drills.

And yet.

In some ways this little anecdote is a helpful way to end our meditation on peace and Ignatian spirituality. There, on that soccer field, where a variety of people gathered to do something quite ordinary in the wake of something utterly overwhelming, we glimpse seeds of peace.

Instead of division, we chose community. Instead of being paralyzed in fear, we left our homes and hit the field. Instead of allowing hatred and vengeance to fester, we turned our attention to something mundane, something we did every week. We focused on each other, on our community, on continuing to muddle through the day-to-day.

At least, for a time. Of course, there were those who could not take time that day to bring their kids to soccer practice. There were those doing heroic work; there were those mourning the dead. And we know all too well what acts of violence and hate were done in the days, weeks, months, and years that followed.

But I offer the image to you all the same: a simple, ordinary group of kids kicking a soccer ball around in spite of global terror. The image is still there, in those mundane moments, where the *magis* breaks through. Where we discover who we are and what we love and why we love it. Where we build and sustain a life worth living, a life worth protecting, a life worth seeing flourish.

These are the moments of peace that make the whole enterprise worthwhile. As Saint Ignatius reminds us, God is in all things. It's easier, sometimes, to see God in the big moments—or to see God's absence in big tragic moments. We certainly turn to God more readily in times of fear or suffering, when violence is knocking at our door. But most of us live the vast majority of our days in the quiet, ordinary, mundane moments of daily life. And sometimes we forget: God is just as present here too.

And God dreams of true peace.

I love speculative stories, tales of fantasy and myth and science fiction. At the end of such stories, our heroes—we *hope*—have found peace. They've vanquished a dragon, fought back the invading army, and brought the mystical talisman to its proper time and place. Then, our heroes just go home. They keep living their lives.

As a kid, I always wondered about those endings. After all the excitement of adventure and battle, wasn't such an ending a letdown? How did they go on with ordinary life when they'd had such an epic journey?

I didn't realize that the newfound peace of the life they returned to was the whole point of the journey—and indeed, that the work wasn't yet finished. The dragon may no longer be breathing fire down villagers' necks, but what about the frayed relationships? The threat of the invaders had been neutralized, but how would the frightened village learn once more to welcome the stranger, to go boldly into new lands as ambassadors of peace? These are quieter stories, more mundane. But just as essential. These are the stories grounded in the slow, steady work of relationship.

I can't know what new conflicts have arisen around the globe since I've written these final words. I can't know what personal battles you find yourself caught in, what violence may have visited your life. But I do know this: The work of peace continues regardless—the work of building up God's dream of peace by building up relationships, by seeing people for who they really are and what they really need, by imagining the seemingly impossible we might yet do, and by forgiving that which has already been done. We invite peace by embracing our unique identity as the beloved of God—and realizing that every person shares in that identity—as well as by making space for God's Spirit to make known our own *magis* and then finding the courage and the community through which to bear its fruits.

Peace is here now, waiting. But we also have work to do. That work begins today in the quiet, the mundane, and the yet-to-be-named-as extraordinary.

Acknowledgments

The seeds for this book were planted by many different people in many different places over a great span of time.

My undergraduate academic mentor at Fairfield University, Dr. Janie Leatherman, was the first to introduce me to the field of peace studies, as well as to the work of John Paul Lederach. She was a great guide and source of support in my fledgling interest in peace, religion, and spirituality. Likewise, my capstone adviser at American University, Dr. Anthony Wanis, was generous enough to entertain my odd-at-times ideas about sacramentality, structural violence, and peacebuilding. He also introduced me to the work of Johan Galtung and guided my writing to a meaningful conclusion.

My former colleagues at Catholic Relief Services, particularly those who did the work of peacebuilding, kindly allowed me to shadow them in their efforts, offering me hours of expertise and insight in my early career days. Though many years have passed, those experiences remain formative.

From the academic to the professional to the personal, I am also grateful to the young adult community at St. Ignatius Catholic Church in Baltimore, who—many years ago, back when I was in fact a young adult—committed to spending an entire Lenten season reflecting on the themes of peace with John Dear's book *Walking the Way: Following Jesus on the Lenten Journey of Gospel Nonviolence to the Cross and Resurrection.*

My friend Shannon Evans encouraged me in the writing of this book and reviewed chapters in both first draft and I-really-hope-this-is-final draft form—thank you. My friend Father Brian Christopher, SJ, also kindly reviewed a number of these chapters to assure me that I was indeed writing in the tradition of Saint Ignatius of Loyola. Thank you to my agent, Keely Boeving, who helped dream up this project and find it a happy home, and to the good folks at Brazos Press, especially Katelyn Beaty, who have shepherded it into the world.

I continue to remain in deep gratitude to my colleagues and collaborators at the Jesuit Conference of Canada and the United States and the Jesuit Media Lab, who accompany me in living out the Ignatian tradition, providing day-to-day experience in what it means to be contemplatives in action.

I am, of course, deeply grateful to my family, who supports me in my writing, my praying, and my dreaming. Thanks to Mom, Dad, Alex, Camira, Elianna, and Alli—especially to Alli, who so often entertains our girls while I try to wrestle with a few additional words and place them in some consequential order on the page. Alli, who so often reminds me to *turn back to peace* in my own life and to *make peace* with those parts of myself that would otherwise prefer conflict. Alli, who happily discusses chapter themes over dinner and who patiently reminds me to be confident in the fact that yes, I am a half-decent writer.

And finally, to my long-time friend and spiritual director, Father Jim Bowler, SJ. Jim walked with me in the spiritual life from my undergraduate days and went home to God while I was about halfway through this manuscript. He was the one who showed me the heart of the Spiritual Exercises and who believed in the promise of this book when it was just a random idea bouncing around in my head. Two months before he died, in the throes of his own cross of suffering and pain, Jim nevertheless insisted I present some of these ideas to his Jesuit community in Massachusetts—that's how much he believed in them, believed in me. Thanks, Jim, for showing me the way to a God who delights.

Notes

Introduction A Prayer for Peace

1. John Dear, *Living Peace: A Spirituality of Contemplation and Action* (Doubleday, 2001), 10.

Chapter 1 God Dreams of More: Discovering Our *Magis*

1. *The Empire Strikes Back*, screenplay by Leigh Brackett and Lawrence Kasdan, directed by Irvin Kershner (Lucasfilm and 20th Century Fox, 1980).

2. Saint Ignatius, *The Spiritual Exercises*, trans. Louis J. Puhl, SJ (Loyola, 1951), 12.

3. Ignatius, *Spiritual Exercises*, 12.

4. John J. English, *Spiritual Freedom: From an Experience of the Ignatian Exercises to the Art of Spiritual Guidance*, 2nd ed. (Loyola University Press, 1995), 269, 262.

5. Pierre Teilhard de Chardin, *Writings*, ed. Ursula King, Modern Spiritual Masters Series (Orbis Books, 1999), 50–51.

6. Saint Irenaeus, *Irenaeus on the Christian Faith: A Condensation of "Against Heresies,"* ed. James Payton (Pickwick, 2011), 116.

7. Ignatius, *Spiritual Exercises*, 11.

8. Pierre Teilhard de Chardin, "Patient Trust," IgnatianSprituality.com, https://www.ignatianspirituality.com/prayer-of-theilhard-de-chardin/. Reprinted with permission.

Chapter 2 Experience Delight: Embracing Our Identity as Beloved

1. *The Sixth Sense*, written and directed by M. Night Shyamalan (Hollywood Pictures, 1999).

2. John J. English, *Spiritual Freedom: From an Experience of the Ignatian Exercises to the Art of Spiritual Guidance*, 2nd ed. (Loyola University Press, 1995), 264.

3. English, *Spiritual Freedom*, 261.

4. English, *Spiritual Freedom*, 264.

5. English, *Spiritual Freedom*, 272.

6. I write at length about this experience in *Cannonball Moments: Telling Your Story, Deepening Your Faith* (Loyola, 2022).

7. Johan Galtung and Graeme MacQueen, *Globalizing God: Religion, Spirituality and Peace* (Transcend University Press, 2008), 34–38.

8. Galtung and MacQueen, *Globalizing God*, 37.

9. English, *Spiritual Freedom*, 271.

10. Galtung and MacQueen, *Globalizing God*, 39.

11. Eric Clayton, host, *AMDG: A Jesuit Podcast*, "Give Thanks the Ignatian Way," with Mark Thibodeaux, SJ," Jesuit Conference of Canada and the United States, November 2023, https://soundcloud.com/jesuitconfer ence/give-thanks-the-ignatian-way-with-mark-thibodeaux-sj.

Chapter 3 Seeing Suffering, Dreaming Peace

1. Walter J. Burghardt, SJ, "Contemplation: A Long Loving Look at the Real," in *An Ignatian Spirituality Reader*, ed. George W. Traub, SJ (Loyola, 2008), 91–93 (emphasis as shown in the original).

2. Burghardt, "Contemplation," 93.

3. Saint Ignatius, *The Spiritual Exercises*, trans. Louis J. Puhl, SJ (Loyola, 1951), 201.

4. "Interreligious Dance," Society of Jesus, February 26, 2020, https://www.youtube.com/watch?v=uBsouvBhj90. Quotations from Amani in the paragraphs that follow are taken from this interview.

5. J. R. R. Tolkien, *Tales from the Perilous Realm* (Mariner Books, 2021), 384.

6. Tolkien, *Tales from the Perilous Realm*, 389.

7. Neil Gaiman, *Coraline* (HarperCollins, 2002), from the opening epigraph.

Chapter 4 Cannonballs, Peace, and the Ignatian Imagination

1. Details about Ignatius's life are from *Ignatius of Loyola: The Spiritual Exercises and Selected Works*, ed. George E. Ganss, SJ (Paulist Press, 1991), 13; and Kevin F. Burke, SJ, and Eileen Burke-Sullivan, *Ignatian Tradition*, Spirituality in History Series (Liturgical Press, 2009), xxiv.

2. *Ignatius of Loyola*, 68.

3. *Ignatius of Loyola*, 69.

4. Eric Clayton, host, *AMDG: A Jesuit Podcast*, "The Ignatian Year Invites Us to Reach Out to Trauma Victims," with Rob McChesney, SJ, Jesuit Conference of Canada and the United States, https://soundcloud

.com/jesuitconference/the-ignatian-year-invites-us-to-reach-out-to-trauma -victims-rob-mcchesney-sj-tells-us-how.

5. Clayton, "The Ignatian Year," with Rob McChesney.

6. John Paul Lederach, *The Moral Imagination: The Art and Soul of Building Peace* (Oxford University Press, 2005), 29.

7. Lederach, *Moral Imagination*, 29.

8. Lederach, *Moral Imagination*, 29.

9. Joseph Campbell, *The Hero with a Thousand Faces*, 3rd ed. (New World Library, 2008), 49.

10. Jessica Brody, *Save the Cat! Writes a Novel: The Last Book on Novel Writing You'll Ever Need* (Ten Speed Press, 2018), 44.

11. Saint Ignatius, *The Spiritual Exercises*, trans. Louis J. Puhl, SJ (Loyola, 1951), 44.

12. Ignatius, *Spiritual Exercises*, 44.

13. John J. English, *Spiritual Freedom: From an Experience of the Ignatian Exercises to the Art of Spiritual Guidance*, 2nd ed. (Loyola House, 1974), 99.

14. Louis M. Savary, *The New Spiritual Exercises: In the Spirit of Pierre Teilhard de Chardin* (Paulist Press, 2010), 74–75.

15. David L. Fleming, SJ, *Like the Lightning: The Dynamics of the Ignatian Exercises* (Institute of Jesuit Sources, 2004), 108.

16. English, *Spiritual Freedom*, 103.

17. Katherine Dyckman, Mary Garvin, and Elizabeth Liebert in *The Spiritual Exercises Reclaimed: Uncovering Liberating Possibilities for Women* (Paulist Press, 2001), 193.

18. Dean Brackley, SJ, *The Call to Discernment in Troubled Times: New Perspectives on the Transformative Wisdom of Ignatius of Loyola* (Crossroad, 2004), 71, 59.

19. Savary, *New Spiritual Exercises*, 74.

20. Brackley, *Call to Discernment*, 66.

21. Lederach, *Moral Imagination*, 173.

Chapter 5 Incarnation: When Peace Draws Near

1. Dr. Seuss, *How the Grinch Stole Christmas* (Random House, 1957), n.p.

2. Saint Ignatius, *The Spiritual Exercises*, trans. Louis J. Puhl, SJ (Loyola, 1951), 49.

3. Ignatius, *Spiritual Exercises*, 49.

4. Ignatius, *Spiritual Exercises*, 50.

5. Robert W. McChesney, "Noticing *Hibakusha*: A Trauma-Informed Reading of the Incarnation Contemplation," *The Way* 62, no. 4 (2023): 52.

6. McChesney, "Noticing *Hibakusha*," 50.

7. Dean Brackley, SJ, *The Call to Discernment in Troubled Times: New Perspectives on the Transformative Wisdom of Ignatius of Loyola* (Crossroad, 2004), 92.

8. Brackley, *Call to Discernment*, 98.

9. Brackley, *Call to Discernment*, 99.

10. Louis M. Savary, *The New Spiritual Exercises: In the Spirit of Pierre Teilhard de Chardin* (Paulist Press, 2010), 86.

11. Savary, *New Spiritual Exercises*, 87.

12. Savary, *New Spiritual Exercises*, 86.

13. Pierre Teilhard de Chardin, *Writings*, ed. Ursula King, Modern Spiritual Masters Series (Orbis Books, 1999), 12.

14. Ursula King, introduction to Teilhard, *Writings*, 18.

15. Teilhard de Chardin, "Attributes of the Universal Christ," in *Writings*, 91.

16. Teilhard, "The Christified Universe," in *Writings*, 116.

17. C. S. Lewis, *The Four Loves* (Harcourt, 1960), 65.

Chapter 6 Two Standards, Two Directions

1. Saint Ignatius, *The Spiritual Exercises*, trans. Louis J. Puhl, SJ (Loyola, 1951), 60.

2. Ignatius, *Spiritual Exercises*, 61.

3. Joseph A. Tetlow, SJ, *Making Choices in Christ: The Foundations of Ignatian Spirituality* (Loyola, 2008), 108.

4. Dean Brackley, SJ, *The Call to Discernment in Troubled Times: New Perspectives on the Transformative Wisdom of Ignatius of Loyola* (Crossroad, 2004), 83.

5. Ignatius, *Spiritual Exercises*, 62.

6. Katherine Dyckman, Mary Garvin, and Elizabeth Liebert, *The Spiritual Exercises Reclaimed: Uncovering Liberating Possibilities for Women* (Paulist Press, 2001), 195.

7. Brackley, *Call to Discernment*, 80.

8. Ronald D. Siegel, *The Extraordinary Gift of Being Ordinary: Finding Happiness Right Where You Are* (Guilford, 2022), 64 (emphasis as shown in the original).

9. Siegel, *Extraordinary Gift*, 66.

10. Ignatius, *Spiritual Exercises*, 62.

11. Brackley, *Call to Discernment*, 80.

12. Christopher S. Collins, SJ, *Habits of Freedom: 5 Ignatian Tools for Clearing Your Mind and Resting Daily in the Lord* (Ave Maria, 2022), 41.

13. Collins, *Habits of Freedom*, 42.

Chapter 7 Structures Built on Sand and Violence

1. *Barbie*, directed and written by Greta Gerwig (Warner Bros., 2023).

2. Johan Galtung and Graeme MacQueen, *Globalizing God: Religion, Spirituality and Peace* (Transcend University Press, 2008), 16 (emphasis added).

3. Galtung and MacQueen, *Globalizing God*, 16.

4. Johan J. Galtung, "Twenty-Five Years of Peace Research: Ten Challenges and Some Responses," *Journal of Peace Research* 22, no. 2 (1985): 145.

5. Johan J. Galtung, "Cultural Violence," *Journal of Peace Research* 27, no. 3 (1990): 291.

6. Galtung and MacQueen, *Globalizing God*, 18.

7. Dean Brackley, SJ, *The Call to Discernment in Troubled Times: New Perspectives on the Transformative Wisdom of Ignatius of Loyola* (Crossroad, 2004), 95.

8. Brackley, *Call to Discernment*, 95.

9. Brackley, *Call to Discernment*, 96.

10. Brackley, *Call to Discernment*, 100.

11. Brackley, *Call to Discernment*, 100–101.

12. Gustavo Gutiérrez, *A Theology of Liberation: History, Politics, and Salvation*, trans. Matthew J. O'Connell (Orbis Books, 1988), 118.

13. Daniel Philpott, "Reconciliation," in *Peacebuilding: Catholic Theology, Ethics, and Praxis*, ed. Robert J. Schreiter, R. Scott Appleby, and Gerard F. Powers (Orbis Books, 2010), 103.

14. Saint Ignatius, *The Spiritual Exercises*, trans. Louis J. Puhl, SJ (Loyola, 1951), 145.

15. Galtung and MacQueen, *Globalizing God*, 37.

16. Ignatius, *Spiritual Exercises*, 145.

17. Ignatius, *Spiritual Exercises*, 145–46.

18. Ignatius, *Spiritual Exercises*, 146.

Chapter 8 Embracing a Spirit of Indifference

1. Saint Ignatius, *The Spiritual Exercises*, trans. Louis J. Puhl, SJ (Loyola, 1951), 64.

2. Ignatius, *Spiritual Exercises*, 65.

3. Ignatius, *Spiritual Exercises*, 12.

Chapter 9 The Nonviolent Christ

1. Saint Ignatius, *The Spiritual Exercises*, trans. Louis J. Puhl, SJ (Loyola, 1951), 81.

2. John Dear, *The Nonviolent Life* (Pace e Bene, 2013), 15.

3. Marie Dennis, ed., *Choosing Peace: The Catholic Church Returns to Gospel Nonviolence* (Orbis Books, 2018), 10.

4. Dennis, *Choosing Peace*, 224–25. The pope's address, titled "Nonviolence: A Style of Politics for Peace," is available in full at https://www.vati can.va/content/francesco/en/messages/peace/documents/papa-francesco _20161208_messaggio-l-giornata-mondiale-pace-2017.html.

5. Dennis, *Choosing Peace*, 24.

6. Dennis, *Choosing Peace*, 11. Butigan and Dear's essay was prepared for participants at the 2016 Nonviolence and Just Peace Conference,

organized by the Pontifical Council for Justice and Peace and Pax Christi International.

7. John Dear, *Walking the Way: Following Jesus on the Lenten Journey of Gospel Nonviolence to the Cross and Resurrection* (Wipf & Stock, 2015), 8.

8. Eric Clayton, "John Lewis and the Genius of Nonviolence," Grotto Network, August 3, 2020, https://www.grottonetwork.com/stories/practice-peace-and-nonviolence.

9. John J. English, *Spiritual Freedom: From an Experience of the Ignatian Exercises to the Art of Spiritual Guidance*, 2nd ed. (Loyola House, 1974), 218.

10. John Paul II, *Sollicitudo rei socialis* (Vatican, 1987), par. 38, https://www.vatican.va/content/john-paul-ii/en/encyclicals/documents/hf_jp-ii_enc_30121987_sollicitudo-rei-socialis.html.

11. Benedict XVI, *Caritas in veritate* (Vatican, 2009), par. 7, https://www.vatican.va/content/benedict-xvi/en/encyclicals/documents/hf_ben-xvi_enc_20090629_caritas-in-veritate.html (emphasis as shown in the original).

12. Francis, *Fratelli tutti* (Vatican, 2020), par. 116, https://www.vatican.va/content/francesco/en/encyclicals/documents/papa-francesco_20201003_enciclica-fratelli-tutti.html.

13. Thich Nhat Hanh, *Being Peace* (Parallax, 1987), 88 (emphasis as shown in the original).

14. English, *Spiritual Freedom*, 222.

15. Dear, *Nonviolent Life*, 5.

Chapter 10 Risen and Returned

1. Maria Isabel Sánchez Vegara, *Mahatma Gandhi*, Little People, Big Dreams 25 (Francis Lincoln Children's Books, 2023), n.p.

2. Sánchez Vegara, *Mahatma Gandhi*, n.p.

3. Joseph Campbell, *The Hero with a Thousand Faces*, 3rd ed. (New World Library, 2008), 23.

4. Saint Ignatius, *The Spiritual Exercises*, trans. Louis J. Puhl, SJ (Loyola, 1951), 95.

5. John J. English, *Spiritual Freedom: From an Experience of the Ignatian Exercises to the Art of Spiritual Guidance*, 2nd ed. (Loyola House, 1974), 231.

6. Pope Francis, *Evangelii gaudium* (Vatican, 2013), par. 6, https://www.vatican.va/content/francesco/en/apost_exhortations/documents/papa-francesco_esortazione-ap_20131124_evangelii-gaudium.html.

7. Ignatius, *Spiritual Exercises*, 132.

8. Ignatius, *Spiritual Exercises*, 133.

9. Ignatius, *Spiritual Exercises*, 96.

10. Ignatius, *Spiritual Exercises*, 95.

11. English, *Spiritual Freedom*, 230.

12. English, *Spiritual Freedom*, 232.

13. Pierre Teilhard de Chardin, *Writings*, ed. Ursula King, Modern Spiritual Masters Series (Orbis Books, 1999), 88.

14. English, *Spiritual Freedom*, 275.

15. Ignatius, *Spiritual Exercises*, 101.

16. Ignatius, *Spiritual Exercises*, 101.

17. English, *Spiritual Freedom*, 276.

18. English, *Spiritual Freedom*, 281–82.

19. John W. O'Malley, *The First Jesuits* (Harvard University Press, 1993), 68.

20. O'Malley, *First Jesuits*, 68.

21. O'Malley, *First Jesuits*, 169.

22. This mission statement is available in the footer of the website for the Jesuits, https://www.jesuits.global.

23. Margaret Silf, *Companions of Christ: Ignatian Spirituality for Everyday Living* (Eerdmans, 2004), 90.

24. Silf, *Companions of Christ*, 91.

25. Ignatius, *Spiritual Exercises*, 6.

Chapter 11 The Spirit of Creativity Brings Peace

1. Robert J. Schreiter, CPPS, "Grassroots Artisans of Peace: A Theological Afterword," in *Artisans of Peace: Grassroots Peacemaking Among Christian Communities*, ed. Mary Ann Cejka and Thomas Bamat (Orbis Books, 2003), 289.

2. Schreiter, "Grassroots Artisans of Peace," 291.

3. Schreiter, "Grassroots Artisans of Peace," 289.

4. John Paul Lederach, *The Moral Imagination: The Art and Soul of Building Peace* (Oxford University Press, 2005), 160.

5. Lederach, *Moral Imagination*, 160.

6. Gerard Manley Hopkins, "God's Grandeur," Poetry Foundation, https://www.poetryfoundation.org/poems/44395/gods-grandeur.

7. Lederach, *Moral Imagination*, 161.

8. Christopher Pramuk, *The Artist Alive: Explorations in Music, Art, and Theology* (Anselm Academic, 2019), 29.

9. Pramuk, *Artist Alive*, 30.

10. Pramuk, *Artist Alive*, 36.

11. Eric A. Clayton, *My Life with the Jedi: The Spirituality of Star Wars* (Loyola, 2023).

Chapter 12 Forgiveness: Broken and Shared

1. *Ignatius of Loyola: The Spiritual Exercises and Selected Works*, ed. George E. Ganss, SJ (Paulist Press, 1991), 77.

2. Saint Ignatius, *The Spiritual Exercises*, trans. Louis J. Puhl, SJ (Loyola, 1951), 154–55.

3. Mary John Mananzan, OSB, "A Theology of Power," in *Artisans of Peace: Grassroots Peacemaking Among Christian Communities*, ed. Mary Ann Cejka and Thomas Bamat (Orbis Books, 2003), 284.

4. Robert J. Schreiter, CPPS., "Grassroots Artisans of Peace: A Theological Afterword," in *Artisans of Peace*, 294.

5. Marina McCoy, *The Ignatian Guide to Forgiveness: Ten Steps to Healing* (Loyola, 2020), 151.

6. McCoy, *Ignatian Guide to Forgiveness*, 152.

7. Carl McColman, *The Little Book of Christian Mysticism: Essential Wisdom of Saints, Seers, and Sages* (Broadleaf Books, 2018), 53.

ERIC CLAYTON is an award-winning writer, speaker, story-teller, and sought-after retreat leader. He is the author of *My Life with the Jedi: The Spirituality of Star Wars*, a book that uses Ignatian spirituality to explore the spiritual underpinnings of a beloved space opera, and *Cannonball Moments: Telling Your Story, Deepening Your Faith*. He is the deputy director of communications at the Jesuit Conference of Canada and the United States, where he guest hosts *AMDG: A Jesuit Podcast* and writes an award-winning weekly newsletter, *Now Discern This*. He has a BA in creative writing and international studies from Fairfield University and an MA in international media from American University. He also has a graduate-level certificate from Creighton University's program in the Ignatian tradition. Eric lives near Baltimore with his family.

Connect with Eric

ericclaytonwrites.com

ericclayton.substack.com

   @eclaytopia